Men of
Modern Architecture

by the author of
FRANK LLOYD WRIGHT: Rebel in Concrete

Giants in Glass,
Steel and Stone

MEN
OF
MODERN
ARCHITECTURE

Aylesa Forsee

MACRAE SMITH COMPANY
PHILADELPHIA

ACKNOWLEDGMENTS

I wish to express my appreciation to the many architects who offered advice, encouragement, and cooperation in the various stages of preparation of this book. Richard Neutra and Walter Gropius, in particular, gave much time and thought to checking the manuscript, steering me to sources of information, and supplying anecdotes.

Foreword

The reader who glances through the Table of Contents may not find the name of a favorite architect. Why, he may ask, were I. Ming Pei, Philip Johnson, Louis I. Kahn, R. Buckminster Fuller, Le Corbusier, Minoru Yamasaki, or others omitted? Part of the answer is that limited space forced selectivity, if the biographies were to be more than mere thumbnail sketches. The author's decision to select only builders who were American by birth or adoption eliminated some.

Another consideration was to have a group of architects through whose lives the reader could trace the evolution of modern architecture. Since Louis Sullivan was first to give artistic form to steel skyscrapers, it seemed logical to start with him. Other architects follow in chronological order.

For this collection, the author wanted some architects who were early starters and some who were late; some who had a college education and some who had the learn-by-doing kind of education. It seemed desirable to include architects who had done some building abroad, and all except Louis Sullivan did.

Variety in output also entered into the decision as to which architects to write about. Richard Neutra, although perhaps best known for homes and schools, has built a number of handsome buildings of many types. Eero Saarinen designed only a few houses, but his public buildings range from laboratories and embassies to the C.B.S. skyscraper in New York City and the

TWA Terminal Building at Kennedy International Airport. And Edward D. Stone has also displayed remarkable versatility in everything from atrium houses to the National Geographic Building in Washington, D.C., and a "pill factory" in Pasadena.

In many instances the lives of these men were intertwined. The career of Frank Lloyd Wright was launched while he was in the office of Louis Sullivan. Richard Neutra was a draftsman for and later a collaborator with Eric Mendelsohn. Mies van der Rohe and Walter Gropius were fellow apprentices in the office of the architect Peter Behrens.

The public tends to judge architects by their products: Do their buildings please the eye? Do they function well in providing warmth and shelter? But in these biographies an attempt has been made to get glimpses of the men behind the buildings. What influence have they exerted on colleagues, apprentices, the public? How did they respond to adversity? Frank Lloyd Wright, for example, in the face of financial setbacks, a home twice destroyed by fire, and personal tragedies, never went down in defeat. Gropius, Mies van der Rohe, Mendelsohn, and Neutra, although their lives were disrupted by war, had the courage to make a new beginning in an alien land.

The men in this book proved themselves to be uncommon architects, but they were also uncommon men.

Contents

Pronunciation Guide

Of the names in this book, Louis Sullivan, Frank Lloyd Wright, and Edward Durrell Stone are easily pronounceable. A key is given below for the pronunciation of those about which there might be some question.

    Walter Gropius—GROW pih us
    Eric Mendelsohn—MEN d'l sun
    Richard Neutra—NOY trah
    Mies van der Rohe—MES vahn der ROHeh
    Eero Saarinen—AR row SAH rih nen

Men of
Modern Architecture

ONE

LOUIS SULLIVAN

Prophet with Little Honor

When he was nineteen, Louis Sullivan aroused comment and criticism for his frescoes at the Moody Tabernacle in Chicago. To do these he had painted colorful leaf and flower designs in freshly spread plaster before it dried. A number of persons who attended the Tabernacle called the frescoes gaudy and threatened to remove them. Someone scrawled on one of the walls, "This is the most disgraceful coloring that ever defiled a church."

But the evangelist Moody accepted Sullivan's work. And the Chicago *Tribune* reported that the imaginative, well-executed frescoes were worth going to see. According to one reporter, young Sullivan showed glowing promise.

Louis' feeling for color and his talent in design had been nurtured by his mother, Andrienne List Sullivan, who excelled both as painter and pianist. During a childhood spent in and around Boston,

13 □

Louis and his older brother Albert often set up easels and painted alongside their mother.

Their father Patrick Sullivan, a dancer by profession, also sketched. But his influence on his sons was exerted more in the development of self-discipline than of art. He enforced a rigorous program that involved cold baths in the morning, long hikes, races, and muscle building.

Louis had much more freedom during the summers on the farm of his maternal grandparents not far from Boston. After vacations spent learning the ways of bullfrogs, turtles, and thrushes, Louis hated to return to crowded city living, school, and piano lessons. To escape the world of adult demands he would go off exploring wharves, alleys, and construction sites. Buildings, he discovered, had personalities. The gleaming Masonic Temple with pinnacles looked joyous, but the State House, despite its golden dome, impressed him as a stingy old woman.

One day in 1868, Louis, then twelve, saw a man of dignified bearing come out of a building, enter a carriage, and signal the coachman to drive away.

"Who was that?" Louis asked a workman standing nearby.

"The man that drawed the plans for the building," the workman replied.

It had never occurred to Louis that buildings came out of people's heads. The idea of making drawings for workmen to follow excited him. Right then and there he decided to become an architect.

Two years later, Louis, still determined to follow architecture as a career, entered English High School in Boston. He particularly liked botany and mineralogy, and in these classes he was constantly on the lookout for the relationship between function and structure.

Louis had been in high school only a short time when his parents moved to Chicago to open a studio for lessons in music and

Louis Sullivan

dancing. Albert went with them, but Louis wanted to finish his education in the East and stayed with his grandparents.

His rugged schedule seemed even worse because he missed his mother's understanding and his brother's companionship. On school days he got up at four o'clock in the morning, walked a mile, often in the snow, to the Wakefield station, and took the train to Boston. There he walked a mile to the place where he ate breakfast, and then trudged another mile to the high school. In the afternoon, when classes were over, he reversed the procedure.

At sixteen, Louis took the entrance examinations for the School of Architecture of the Massachusetts Institute of Technology and won admission. In the lecture room, he soon learned that columns belonged to Classic architecture, spires to Gothic; and in the drafting room, his drawing improved under the guidance of Professor William Ware. Louis liked M.I.T. well enough, but he longed to go to that famous school for artists and architects, the Ecole des

Beaux-Arts in Paris. His parents approved this goal but insisted that he must be more than sixteen before he studied abroad.

At the end of a year at M.I.T., Louis went to Philadelphia because his grandfather had moved there after Mrs. List's death to make his home with his son Jules. Among the buildings he saw, Louis most admired a house designed by Frank Furness. He went immediately to apply for a job at the office of this architect and his partner Hewitt. Furness, a red-bearded man who wore a flashy plaid suit and a scowl, asked a number of questions.

Finally he said, "Come tomorrow for a trial as draftsman, but I prophesy that you won't last a week."

Louis *did* last, and Furness turned out to be kind despite his initial gruffness. As he shared his beliefs about architecture, Furness continually stressed that a building should proclaim its use.

That fall, in the panic of 1873, business and bank failures multiplied, and commissions stopped coming to the office. One morning in November, Furness told Louis, "I wish you might stay. But as you were the last to come, it is only right that you should be the first to go."

Discouraged by the loss of his job, lonely for his brother and parents, Louis thought it would be best to go to Chicago for Thanksgiving and try to find work there. Although forewarned, he was shocked at the expanse of gutted ruins and gray shanties—aftermath of the Great Fire of 1871. But he could see that there would be a bright future here for builders.

Louis found a job as draftsman in the office of Major William Le Baron Jenney. The Major was more of an engineer than an architect, but what he knew he taught well. Louis also learned much from the youthful office foreman, John Edelman, and a friendship sprang up between them.

John introduced Louis and his brother Albert to the Lotos Club, a group of boat owners who had a club with headquarters on

the Calumet River. Weekends, members competed in rowing, swimming, track, and field events. Nights they slept in their boathouses.

Louis liked Chicago, his job, and outings with Lotos Club
friends, but if he meant to go to the Ecole des Beaux-Arts, he thought
he should be about it, since he was almost eighteen. On July 10,
1874, he left New York aboard the *Britannica* bound for Paris via
London.

In Paris, Louis found quarters on the seventh floor of a room-
ing hotel in the Latin Quarter. The room, up a hundred and fourteen
steps from the street, had very little furniture, but a tiny balcony
opened toward the famous Notre Dame Cathedral. He could share
cheap meals with other roomers—mostly students.

Louis had only six weeks to prepare for a battery of examinations that would cover a wide range of subjects and extend over a
three-week period. Oral interviews would be in French. In high
school, Louis had taken a first prize in French, but here among
natives he had trouble making himself understood. He arranged for
a tutor in French and another in mathematics. Daytimes, he allowed
himself only short breaks for meals and exercise. Nights, by candle-
light, he studied French, read history, and organized notes taken in
tutorial sessions.

During the weeks of testing he earned high scores and gained
entrance to the Ecole. He began his training in the workshop or
atelier of M. Emil Vaudremer. Vaudremer disciplined his students,
but his criticisms were just and Louis respected and liked him. While
working on an assigned project, designing an original room, Louis
gained sureness in the use of pencil and triangle.

But Paris was not all books, designs, and drawing pencils.
With atelier companions, Louis relaxed in the Jardins du Luxem-
bourg, visited monuments, museums, and architectural exhibitions,
went to a costume ball, and danced.

Beaux-Arts students could work away from the atelier if they

17 □

wished, provided they met the deadline for their current project. This gave Louis a chance to go to Italy. By the time he returned to Paris, architectural history had come alive for him.

During the spring, Louis became increasingly dissatisfied with the Beaux-Arts program. Ideas pushed his pencil into creating original designs, but his teachers insisted on formulas and on the imitation of old styles. Louis wanted to test his newly developed skills on real buildings instead of artificial projects. Besides that, he was heart-hungry for his family.

Louis returned to the Sullivan home in Chicago in March, 1875. Architects there looked upon his Beaux-Arts education as new-fangled and impractical. He found only minor, temporary jobs in one office after another.

In his spare time, Louis haunted the Lotos Club. Between rowing and racing, John Edelman pushed him into reading good books. Together the two friends dissected leaves and flowers, looking for principles of form and structure that they could apply to architecture. John's critical evaluations helped Louis improve his designs, and engagements grew longer, but no really good opening came his way.

Louis Sullivan was almost twenty-three when he got a position as draftsman in the office of the outstanding architect Dankmar Adler. His first important assignment was to design the ornament for the block of buildings which included the Grand Opera House owned by William Borden. Adler sometimes asked for revision of his designs, but this helped Louis correct his weaknesses.

Incessant work left little time for recreation, but Sullivan was making new friends among the many young architects attracted to Chicago after the Great Fire. At Kinsley's Restaurant where they habitually met for lunch there were daily debates. Sullivan insisted that form should follow function, just as it did in nature. An oak tree always expressed oak function. Why shouldn't the form of a building show its use?

Sullivan got a reputation as a radical because he wanted to get away from historical styles of architecture and create an American style. If a thousand called him wrong he would not change his course. Red-haired John Wellborn Root, who was rapidly making a name in architecture, often came to Sullivan's defense. Adler too supported his ideas and, after Sullivan had been with the firm less than two years, invited him to form a partnership.

The two men worked well together. Adler, an engineer and technician, was especially well equipped to oversee construction. Design was Sullivan's strongest point, and in this area he took the initiative and had the final say.

Sullivan often shared his recreation as well as his work with Adler. In the home of Dankmar and his wife Dila he played piano, romped with the children, and drew pictures for them.

To be closer to the office and his work, Sullivan had moved away from home, but family ties were still strong and it was a blow when his father died June 15, 1884. Although his father had been strict, Louis was grateful that he had instilled self-discipline and courage in his sons.

By the time he was thirty, Sullivan was gaining some recognition both at home and abroad. On November 17, 1886, he addressed the third annual Convention of the Western Architects in Chicago. Although junior to most of the three hundred men assembled, he held their attention with comments on organic architecture. "Life is organic," he told the architects. "It grows, develops, unfolds. Architecture too must unfold form after form."

That same year Albert Sullivan, who had been winning promotions with the Illinois Central, became superintendent of the railway, a position that took him to Cairo, Illinois. This was a loss for Louis, who for years had shared books, friends, fun, and problems with Albert. He was also deprived of the companionship of his mother, who went to stay with her sister Jenny at Lyons Falls, New York.

But Louis had too much to do to brood over his loneliness. Business was booming, and he and Adler were adding to their staff. Almost half of the structures the partners worked on were residences. But they also designed theaters, factories, warehouses, railroad stations, a library, a synagogue, a school, and a series of office buildings, including the Dexter Building.

These buildings attracted attention because they had less massiveness than older ones and opened up more window space, but much of their uniqueness lay in Sullivan's ornamentation. Usually he borrowed his designs from nature—flowers, palmettos, leaves. As he strove for individuality, he sometimes overdid ornamentation, but his friend John Root helped him develop more simplicity.

Sullivan's biggest chance to prove his worth came with the Chicago Auditorium Building. Plans called for an auditorium, larger than any in the country, to be surrounded by a four-hundred-room hotel and offices. A steering committee headed by influential Ferdinand Peck kept calling for revisions. They insisted on such a luxurious interior that Adler and Sullivan had to economize on the exterior. The result was a severe, clifflike building unrelieved except by an arched triple door and a seventeen-story tower. The three lower stories were of granite, the remaining ones of gray-buff limestone.

Sullivan designed the lavish lobby, the dining rooms, and stairways for the hotel. Originality, delicacy, and color characterized the marble floors, stenciled ceiling patterns, and ornamental bands or friezes at the tops of walls. The stairway leading to the second floor had onyx panels, wrought-iron handrails, and mosaic floors on the landings.

For the Auditorium, Sullivan used a skylight of stained glass. Forty boxes at the sides had fronts of cast iron decorated in ivory and gold, the prevailing color scheme of the theater. Ivory plush draperies and chairs upholstered in yellow satin added elegance. Sullivan was swamped when it came to working out details for

Auditorium Building, Chicago, Illinois, by Adler and Sullivan. 1890. View of main foyer, second floor. Photograph courtesy The Museum of Modern Art.

eye-filling ornaments—arches with gold-leaf design, gold rosettes, floral and foliage motifs. To lighten the load he hired Frank Lloyd Wright, a slim lad of eighteen, as an assistant.

Before completion of the building, Adler and Sullivan moved their offices into the Tower. Opening of the Auditorium on the night of December 9, 1889, was a gala affair. Benjamin Harrison, President of the United States, gave a brief address, and Adelina Patti, idol of operagoers, sang. What pleased Louis most was that his brother Albert had come from Cairo, Illinois, for the festivities.

Next day the press praised Adler's engineering and Sullivan's genius in ornamentation. Adler, Sullivan, and the Auditorium became topics of national conversation. Commissions deluged the firm, but the partners were too tired to tackle them. During the three years it had taken to design and build the Auditorium, both men had been under terrific strain.

Adler suggested that Sullivan go to Pueblo and Salt Lake City to check on the progress of the opera houses they had underway there and then take a vacation. Sullivan, who loved to travel, jumped at the chance. In Ocean Springs, Mississippi, he met his Chicago friends, Mr. and Mrs. James Charnley. They were so fascinated by the woods fronting on Biloxi Bay that they bought a tract of land densely forested with oaks, maples, eucalypti, and magnolias. Sullivan drew up designs for a cottage for the Charnleys and one for himself.

The sea breezes and the slower pace of life soothed Sullivan's taut nerves, and he was eager to get back to his work. In Chicago he and Adler plunged into the designing of theaters, synagogues, warehouses, office buildings, and hotels that included the Victoria Hotel in Chicago and the St. Nicholas in St. Louis.

While Sullivan was in St. Louis, wealthy, amiable Ellis Wainwright talked to him about designing a combination store and office building. "It must embody skyscraper design but still be artistic," Wainwright specified.

□ 22

Auditorium Building, Chicago, Illinois. 1890. View of Auditorium interior: organ grille, north side. Photograph courtesy The Museum of Modern Art.

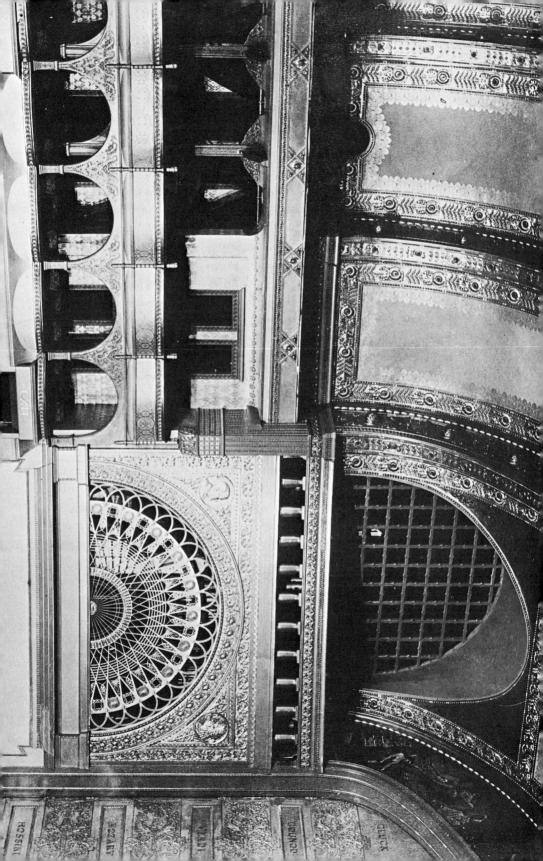

Sullivan reveled in the challenge Wainwright had given him, but even after he got back to Chicago he could not create a design that suited him. The idea of using a steel skeleton in multistory buildings had originated only recently. Skyscrapers thus far had looked much like smaller buildings stacked on top of one another.

One day, while discussing the problem with his assistant, Frank Lloyd Wright, Sullivan asked him, "What is the chief characteristic of a tall building?" Then, without giving him a chance to answer, he continued, "It is lofty. This loftiness is its thrilling aspect."

As he thought about this later, Sullivan realized that architects in general had considered height a liability. Builders could go on fighting height; he was going to accept it. He would make the Wainwright Building a proud and soaring thing. Swept by the urge to pencil his dream, he rushed to his drawing board. He sketched a U-shaped building in which verticality would be stressed through the use of uniformly spaced piers that extended from the third story to the top floor.

The completed Wainwright Building had two lower stories of red granite with no ornament except narrow bands framing the doors. The plain sandstone façade of the upper stories expressed the feeling of a commercial purpose. But there was artistry in line and proportion. Sullivan enriched the top story with ornamentation in red terra-cotta clayware, having the surface coated with a fine glaze. The building won accolades. One reporter called it a poetic expression of metallic frame construction. Sullivan said a new need had called forth a new form.

Another fine accomplishment was redesigning and redecorating the McVickers Theater, in Chicago, the interior of which had been ruined by fire. The Getty Tomb, in Chicago's Graceland Cemetery, for which Sullivan combined gray limestone, ornamental bronze and glass with beauty and balance, was widely publicized.

Pressure of his work left Sullivan little time for diversion, but frequently at night he and Wright would sit together in the tower of the Auditorium and talk as they looked out over the lighted city. Sullivan often quoted poetry or philosophized.

"The true function of the architect," he told Wright, "is to initiate such buildings as shall correspond to the real needs of the people who use them. The architect should impart to the buildings the best that is in people."

Trips, as well as night-time chats, helped Sullivan to unwind. Adler did not like to travel and commissioned his partner to do out-of-town jobs. Because of his brother's superintendency of the Illinois Central, Louis could get free passes, and at intervals he retreated to his Mississippi cottage near Ocean Springs. There he cleared underbrush, designed rose gardens, or planned a pool with a fountain and a pool for crabs, in which he had a special interest.

Sullivan needed all the reserve strength such a vacation had given him when he began to wrestle with the problems presented by the Schiller Building, in Chicago. Although its major function was to house German opera, it was also to include offices and clubrooms.

In the end, Sullivan shielded ground entrances with a canopy of ornamental iron. A balcony ran across the entire front of the second story. The ninth story had a rich terra-cotta frieze, and the seventeenth story was decorated with panels of ornament enclosing arcades. Of special interest was a setback system of the stories, to give a maximum of light. Sullivan's future looked bright. Tall office buildings were much in demand, and he and Adler had proved that they could build them superbly.

Not all of Sullivan's buildings were uniformly good. The press of work kept him from giving enough personal attention. There were disappointments along the way too. When the Templars wanted a fraternity building, he drafted one of the boldest and loftiest ever conceived. But the ambition of the Templars had exceeded their funds, and it remained only on paper and in Sullivan's heart.

But most buildings he sketched became a reality. Early in 1893

25 □

a pet project was a house he and Albert, again a resident of Chicago, had under way for their mother, who was still in the East. The house had been designed to meet every need of a semi-invalid artist, and the brothers were looking forward to her arrival when word came on May 15, 1892, that she had died.

Louis and Albert were so heartsick that neither wanted to live in the house. But Louis finally moved in, installing his piano, books, and bric-a-brac. Oriental art had become a hobby, and Louis owned hand-woven rugs, vases, bronzes, figurines, and a fine collection of jade.

As the Columbian Exposition of 1893 drew near, Sullivan gave most of his attention to the Transportation Building he had been asked to design. He was bitterly disappointed because the planning committee had decided that everything must be classical in style. Sullivan, after pointing out that exposition architecture would be widely copied and would set patterns for years to come, had made a plea for an American kind of architecture but had been ignored.

His assistant Wright, who had become a topnotch architect and a personal friend, shared his views and plans. But then Sullivan discovered that Wright had been carrying on a small private practice in his spare time. To Sullivan this seemed disloyal and unethical. When he rebuked Wright, Wright became angry and resigned his position.

Lonely and disturbed, Sullivan finished the Transportation Building without help except for some consultation with Adler. Because of exposition regulations it had to be white, classical in style, cheap, and capable of rapid construction. But Sullivan designed a great "Golden Door" that incorporated forty-seven distinct ornamental patterns. In the central cupola there was an observation tower reached by elevators. Exhibits set off by brightly colored walls included everything connected with transportation—Conestoga wagons, sedan chairs, balloons, railway locomotives. A second part of the building at the back was a steel-framed, earth-hugging section which housed four complete trains.

□ 26

Guaranty Building, Buffalo, New York, by Louis Sullivan. 1894–1895. Photograph courtesy John Szarkowski. Copyright 1956 by the University of Minnesota.

Critics said the building was little more than a shed and described the "Golden Door" as an unhappy zigzag of scrolls. But many praised Sullivan's boldness and originality. M. André Bouilbet, who represented the Union Centrale des Arts Décoratifs of Paris, asked for drawings, photographs, and models of the building and the "Golden Door" to exhibit in the Museum of Decorative Arts in Paris. Later, this organization awarded Sullivan three medals. From Paris the exhibit traveled to art galleries in Russia, Finland, and elsewhere.

Meanwhile Sullivan and Adler forged ahead. The Guaranty Building in Buffalo, New York, had a rich play of surface ornament. Inside the building, Sullivan achieved elegance with mosaic floors, marble walls, friezes, and wrought-iron stairways. Many thought Sullivan had outdone himself on this building, in which steel and terra-cotta had sprung to life.

Between 1890 and 1894, Sullivan had designed forty buildings, but in 1895 no commissions came at all. A depression that had begun ten years earlier caused bank and business failures and country-wide unemployment. Sullivan was greatly distressed when he and Adler had to dismiss most of their staff of fifty draftsmen and engineers. In July, Adler told him he was withdrawing from the firm to get a job that would guarantee a livelihood for his family.

For Sullivan this was a calamity. His genius had supplied the designs, but although he was almost thirty-nine he knew little about the world of business. Without Adler, the firm would have no guide, no engineer—but worse than that, Sullivan would miss his friend's kindness and generosity. Through the years, each had brought out the best in the other.

Sullivan kept the office, maintained a small staff, and continued to design on manila paper stretched on a drawing board. Deprived of Adler's support he turned more and more to his talented assistant George Elmslie, a shy, tractable, blue-eyed Scot.

Sullivan's first big commission after Adler left was the Bayard

Building in New York. On this he collaborated with the young architect, Lyndon Smith. Some of his colleagues thought Sullivan over-embellished the Bayard Building. Angels with outspread wings placed along the top story did not fit with the rest of the building. But a number of foreign architects called it the best skyscraper yet erected.

After the Bayard Building only minor commissions came Sullivan's way. With more leisure than he'd ever had in his life, he would have enjoyed spending time with his brother, but Albert had married a possessive woman who resented the family tie, and the two men saw each other only infrequently. Because she wanted to live in the home the brothers had built for their mother, Louis moved out of it, but with reluctance.

A new interest eased his loss of Albert's companionship. One day, while out for a stroll, he met a statuesque woman with dark brown eyes and hair combed into a pompadour. She had a dog on a leash, and Sullivan made a comment about the pet. This led to an acquaintanceship. Sullivan soon learned that Margaret Hattabough, twenty-seven years younger than he, was a civil service employee who had been married but was now a divorcée. He was much attracted to her, and they were married July 1, 1900.

Now that Sullivan had a wife to support, it was very important to him to have steady employment, but the busy architects were the ones who imitated the classic style of the Great White City of the Columbian Exposition. This Sullivan would not do.

When only a few clients asked for the kind of building he wanted to design, he became enthusiastic about playing the role of a teacher. A number of young architects, including his assistants George Elmslie and William Gray Purcell, admired him and listened willingly to his monologues.

"Never doubt the possibilities of your own mind," Sullivan told them. When questioned as to where thoughts came from, he said, "Thinking must rest upon an appreciation of the Infinite."

For a year, from February 16, 1901, to February 8, 1902, Sullivan addressed himself to the youth of the land in a series of page-length articles which appeared each week in the *Interstate Architect and Builder*. Entitled "Kindergarten Chats," they took the form of a series of dialogues between an imaginary teacher and pupil.

Sullivan discussed the forms and functions of architecture, but he also had much to say about the architect himself. Any work, he asserted, was an expression of the thoughts and feelings of the artist who created it. The architect must avoid insincere and pretentious actions.

Around 1903 Sullivan was working on the Crane Building in Chicago and also on the Schlesinger and Mayer Building, for which he had designed the first unit four years earlier. His ornamentation gave the latter building a festive impression unusual for a department store. At street level, big windows garnished with lacy metal flowers, vines, and berries invited the passerby inside. After Carson, Pirie, Scott and Company bought the store, another unit was added, but the company employed architect Daniel Burnham, not Sullivan.

Disappointments multiplied in his personal as well as his professional life. At Ocean Springs his wife Margaret was not interested in his hobbies of rose culture and photography. In Chicago she enjoyed social life while he preferred to concentrate on his work or fraternize with friends who would talk about architecture. Frustrated, Sullivan drank coffee and alcohol excessively. When his income dwindled and he and Margaret had to move to cheaper quarters, she lost hope in their future and they separated.

Sullivan had some income from designs for several houses and small stores, but he could no longer afford to keep the Ocean Springs cottage that had been such a delight. He let his art collection go and finally sold rugs, tapestries, statuettes, and books at an auction. Of his jade collection he retained only one exquisitely carved piece. But he clung to his office in the Auditorium and maintained a skeleton staff.

With this staff he designed a bank for the small town of Owatonna, Minnesota. Walls of sandstone and shale brick gave a dark, rich red effect and were ornamented by bronze-green terra-cotta and blue glass mosaic with touches of green, white, and gold.

The success of the Owatonna Bank brought commissions for others in Grinnell, Iowa, Newark, Ohio, and West Lafayette, Indiana. When a contract would come along, Sullivan would be encouraged and expand his staff. Even when he had no prospects, he retrenched as little as possible and refused to compromise. At Sidney, Ohio, directors of the Savings and Loan Association Bank looked dubious when he explained his plan for a skylight of incandescent mother-of-pearl color, tremendous leaded-glass windows, and brilliant glass-mosaic ornament.

"I had rather fancied columns and a little more classicism," said one of the directors.

"Any one of a thousand architects could design the kind of bank you evidently have in mind." Sullivan rolled up his sketch and started to leave.

"Don't be hasty," someone urged. After consultation, the directors accepted Sullivan's plan.

Sullivan considered this bank the best of the series. The exterior, with bricks of rich, varied colors, looked like tapestry rising above the two-foot base of veined, almost black, marble. Over the entrance façade, heraldic lions were modeled in dull-green terra-cotta.

All of Sullivan's banks had been unique. Colorful, gay, lyric, they stood out like jewels on the main streets of their communities. These buildings made him the subject of feature articles, and he was often invited to speak at meetings of architects. But because the banks were in small towns, they received less recognition than they deserved, and only a few clients sought him out.

Between the far-apart commissions, Sullivan wrote. In *Democracy: A Man-Search* he called our form of government the ideal system. It failed, he said, only because men failed to perfect themselves in love, character, and individual responsibility. No publishers were willing to publish the manuscript. Sullivan also revised "Kindergarten

Chats" and put them in book form, but this manuscript too was rejected. The rebuff was harder to take because he was now alone in the Tower office. His assistants had been faithful and loyal, but, unable to live on what Sullivan could pay them, they had resigned one by one. Embittered by a sense of failure, Sullivan paced about his office asking himself why he had been denied the chance to build.

Others, too, asked why Sullivan had been so neglected. The eminent Swedish painter Anders Zorn, on a visit to the United States, queried, "What is wrong with you in Chicago? There in the Auditorium Tower sits your country's greatest living architect, one of the world's leaders in his profession, doing nothing!"

By January, 1918, Sullivan could no longer afford the rent for his large office and moved to small dingy rooms on the second floor of the Auditorium. Two years later he could not even meet the rental there. As he left this office Sullivan could hardly bear the thought of never returning to the building he had designed, the building that had become a landmark and the talk of the nation.

His personal affairs had gone as badly as his career. He had lived in a succession of hotels, each cheaper and shabbier than the last. Personal possessions had shrunk to little more than a few books, handsomely cut but frayed suits, unframed pictures cut out of magazines, and his one piece of jade. Poor health, in part due to excesses to which underwork had led him, often left him feeling spent, dreary, and listless. His brother Albert had gone completely out of his life after a move to the East.

But friends made Sullivan's lot bearable. George Elmslie, Frank Lloyd Wright, with whom the rift had long since been healed, and many others offered companionship. When he was well enough, Sullivan went daily to the Cliff Dwellers Club where friends had provided him with permanent membership. A number of architects ate there regularly. In any group Sullivan joined he could always count on being invited to sit at the head of the table, and he still spoke with eloquence. On a night when the discussion turned to beauty, Sullivan said, "One does not learn to create beauty; one becomes the kind of person who can create beauty." Genius, he insisted, was not a strange thing apart from man. If men would make constant use of the powers given to them, there would be more of so-called genius.

He renewed the use of his own powers when architects Max Dunning and George Nimmons urged him to design a set of twenty plates to illustrate his philosophy of ornament. The Burnham Library of the Chicago Art Institute advanced five hundred dollars toward the project, and Cliff Dweller friends subscribed another five hundred. The Press of the American Institute of Architects asked for publication rights.

Although his hand was shaky, he still drew with speed and certainty. The task, joyous at first, turned burdensome because of neuritis in his right arm, but he finished the delicate designs and sent them off to the engraver.

He then concentrated on an autobiographical series of articles for the *American Institute of Architects Journal,* with the idea that the articles might later be reprinted in book form. The title of the book, Sullivan told his friends, would be *Autobiography of an Idea,* because he regarded his career as the working out of an idea.

Publication of the biographical articles brought requests for others, but Sullivan was not well enough to write much. In the spring of 1924 his condition worsened. He doubted that he would ever see his autobiography or his philosophy of ornament in book form.

One day Max Dunning came to visit him. "I brought you two books," he said.

Sullivan momentarily forgot his pain and weariness when he saw the titles—*Autobiography of an Idea* and *A System of Architectural Ornament.* Enthusiasm mounted as he leafed through them. "Beautiful!" he kept exclaiming.

With royalties from these books, he thought, he would no longer need to depend on friends for his livelihood. And after he was gone, his words, his drawings, would still be here to challenge young architects. His life had not been lived in vain.

On April 13, Sullivan fell into a deep sleep from which he never wakened. He died the next day.

Louis Sullivan was gone, but he had left his mark on downtown Chicago, and elsewhere lofty buildings and gemlike banks gave proof of his talent for uniting realism and romance.

In a sense, Louis Sullivan was our first modern architect. He it was who gave artistic form to the steel-framed skyscraper. Frank Lloyd Wright wrote, "While America's architects were stumbling at its height, piling one thing on top of another, foolishly denying it, Louis Sullivan seized its height as its characteristic feature and made it sing—a new thing under the sun!"

Awards and recognition that would have meant much to Louis Sullivan came too late. *Kindergarten Chats* and *Democracy: A Man-Search,* once rejected, were published after his death. His ideas were circulated by articles and books about him and by architects of the Chicago School.

In 1943, the American Institute of Architects posthumously awarded him its Gold Medal, the highest architectural award in this country.

In 1946, architects of Massachusetts, on the site but not on the house in which Sullivan had lived, affixed a memorial: "Architect and author, whose stalwart and vital achievements mark the beginning of an independent architecture consistent with the normal creative spirit of man, and with the free aspirations of the people of America."

Ten years later, on the hundredth anniversary of Sullivan's birth, the Chicago Art Institute staged a dazzling pictorial exhibit of his work and offered tributes in his memory. In 1964 a citizen's group in Chicago, under the sponsorship of the Auditorium Theater Council, organized to raise funds to restore the long-neglected Auditorium Theater.

Honors have come at last to the prophet so little honored during his own lifetime.

TWO

FRANK LLOYD WRIGHT

Uncommon Architect, Uncommon Man

There was much in the childhood of Frank Lloyd Wright that nudged him in the direction of architecture and unusual achievements. His mother Anna Lloyd-Jones Wright, convinced that her son was destined to become an architect, bought him educational toys invented by the German Friedrich Froebel. These taught Frank to look for patterns of construction and stimulated his sensitivity to materials and to color. His father William Russell Cary Wright, who alternated between music and the ministry, introduced Frank to structures of sound. During piano practice periods, mistakes brought penalties—usually raps on the knuckles. Both parents exposed Frank and his younger sisters Jane and Maginel to the virtues of integrity and hard work.

From the age of eleven, Frank spent his summers working on the farm of his Uncle James in a valley close to Spring Green, Wisconsin. At that time his parents were living in Madison, Wisconsin, where Mr. Wright had opened a conservatory of music. At first, weeding the garden, feeding pigs, and milking cows left Frank continually tired and rebellious. But during successive summers his muscles strengthened and he took pride in his ability to work long hours at men's tasks. Closeness to the land and growing things heightened his awareness for color and form.

During the winters in Madison, Frank treasured the hours when he could retreat to his attic room to draw and design or read about building and builders. But he liked to be with people too and looked forward to the nights when he, his family, and their friends made music together.

Frank and his friend Robert "Robie" Lamp set type on a small printing press in the basement, invented an ice boat, prowled along the lake shore. Forays often ended at some construction site where they watched workmen change stone, lumber, and glass into buildings.

Frank was alone the day he saw the Wisconsin State Capitol collapse while still under construction. Most of the forty workers were killed. The tragedy gave Frank nightmares. Later, he heard that the roof and floors had given way because the contractor had filled the hearts of piers with defective materials. Frank vowed that anything he built would be solid and honest.

Chances for getting the training he needed to become an architect dimmed when Mr. Wright's conservatory did not pay off. Debts piled up during Maginel's long illness. There had always been a great deal of friction between Frank's parents, but now the tension increased. To escape it, Mr. Wright left home. No letters came, no clues as to his whereabouts.

Frank, automatically head of the family, tried to help support his sisters and his mother, who planned to return to teaching. He sold wooden novelties that he turned out on a scroll saw and got a job as assistant in the office of Allen D. Conover, Dean of Engineering at the University of Wisconsin. Because Mrs. Wright insisted

Frank Lloyd Wright

that Frank should have an education, he also enrolled at the university.

The job and his studies ate up most of Frank's hours but he boxed, read a great deal, and shared in the modest activities of Phi Delta Theta fraternity. Frank soon tired of collegiate routines. The university had no school of architecture, and his classes did not seem worth the two-mile hike to the campus and the loss of wages he could have earned in those hours. The office, too, was a disappointment because Conover was more of an engineer than an architect.

It would make more sense, Frank thought, to go to Chicago where he was sure he could find a job in an architectural office and make money to send home while he learned his profession. His mother, however, was determined that he should get his degree first.

37 □

Besides that, she worried about what would happen to his clothes, diet, and morality in the city.

"Uncle Jenkin Lloyd-Jones would be there," Frank reminded her. But when his mother wrote to Uncle Jenkin, then pastor of All Souls Church, he too opposed the move. Frank made up his mind to go anyway. To get money for his expenses he pawned some of his books and the fur collar of his overcoat.

Although he stayed at a cheap hotel in Chicago and ate little except buns and bananas, Frank's funds soon dwindled to twenty cents. He knew the emptiness both of hunger and of fear after he found no opening in any architectural office where he applied. But just as he had almost given up hope, he got a job as tracer—tracing designs, patterns, and drawings for blueprint reproduction—in the office of Joseph Lyman Silsbee.

Temporarily, because his Uncle Jenk insisted, he stayed in the Lloyd-Jones home. There he met stimulating persons and had the companionship of his cousin Richard, as witty as he was intelligent. Later, Frank's mother and his two sisters came to Chicago and the family lived together.

As he went back and forth between the office and their home in Oak Park, Frank studied houses. It bothered him that so many were poorly built or ugly. People ought to have beautiful places in which to live. Architecture, he thought, should come from the heart and be the best one could give. Yet at the office, Silsbee was satisfied with slipshod methods of building.

Frank hesitated to leave the office because he liked Silsbee personally and had learned a great deal from him about the uses of material. And he would miss working with fellow employee Cecil Corwin, who shared his interest in music and architecture and had become a close friend. But Frank got to the point where he could not go on doing what seemed false. Shortly before he was nineteen he applied for and got a position at the well-known firm of Adler and Sullivan.

Fellow draftsmen looked upon Frank as a young upstart and made life miserable for him. Sullivan, gruff and critical, summoned him to his office repeatedly with the cry of "Wright! Wright!"

Because his experiences here would bring him closer to his goal, Wright was willing to endure the hostility of the office force and the imperiousness of his employer. As he worked on designs for the Chicago Auditorium, he maneuvered pencil and T square with new skill. Sullivan began to treat him as an equal. When the firm moved into offices in the Auditorium, Sullivan gave Wright, then twenty-one, a glass cubicle next to his own and assigned him the young draftsman George Elmslie as an assistant.

Sullivan often kept Frank after office hours to talk about books, buildings, music, and philosophy. Architecture, he said, must be honest, individual, and a product of its times. One day, encouraged by Sullivan's friendliness, Wright confided that he had fallen in love with Catherine Tobin, whom he had met at a social at All Souls Church. She had a great deal of charm and shared many of his interests. He wanted to marry her, but he wasn't earning enough to build a home for her.

"I'll lend you the money," Sullivan offered. "You can pay me back through salary deductions over a period of five years."

Wright was elated. He bought a lot in Oak Park and went ahead with plans for a modest house with a pyramid-shaped roof and hovering eaves. To make a place for his mother, he renovated a little cottage already on the property.

Frank and Catherine were married in 1890 and within the first year had a son named Lloyd. Wright considered himself fortunate to have a wife who was a delightful companion, a son, a home built to his own tastes, and a congenial employer, but after the birth of his second son, John, he had financial difficulties.

To help provide for his expanding family, Wright used his spare time to design houses for his own clients. The Charnley and Harlan houses had so much individualty that other commissions came his way. He could take only a few of them because he and Sullivan were hard at work on the Transportation Building for the Columbian Exposition.

Wright was exuberant on the spring day that he went into Sullivan's office to make the final payment on his Oak Park house and to claim the deed on it. Unexpectedly Sullivan refused to give him his contract.

"By designing houses on your own time you violated our agreement," Sullivan told him. He pointed to a passage in fine print that Wright had overlooked.

"I often work overtime for the firm." Wright defended himself. "Why can't I work overtime for myself?"

"I want no division of efforts," Sullivan told him icily.

When Sullivan refused to give him the deed, Wright left the office. Later, because he did not want to lose Sullivan's friendship, he forced himself to return to try to make things right. But as soon as Wright tried to speak, Sullivan told him, "There is nothing I care to hear you say."

In Wright's mind a sense of guilt and humiliation collided with hurt feelings and resentment at what he considered an injustice. Too stunned to reply, he turned and walked out of Sullivan's office. What he would do now he did not know. How could he pay his bills when he was unemployed and was not legally in possession of his home?

A short time later, Adler, whom Wright had always admired for his generosity and honesty, mailed the deed to him, but the break with Sullivan robbed him of some of the pleasure of ownership. By this time, he had made up his mind to go into business on his own. To cut down on rent he persuaded his friend Cecil Corwin to share a suite of rooms with him in the Schiller Building.

Wright's first client there was the wealthy businessman William H. Winslow, who wanted a home at River Forest. The first story was of brick, the second of tile. The roof of terra-cotta tiles, much like a low-pitched lid, hovered over the house. The masterful handling of horizontal lines, the terra-cotta frieze, and the richness of texture attracted viewers.

Wright was more than willing to answer questions about the Winslow House and about his architectural ideas. He frequently used the words *organic architecture.* "In organic architecture," he explained, "everything is interrelated. The whole is to the part as the part to the whole."

After Corwin moved to the East, Wright was so lonely that he joined a group of architects at the Steinway Building. Occasionally the Steinway Hall architects went out to speak to clubs. On a chilly evening in March, Wright delivered an address at Hull House to the Arts and Crafts Society. "The machine is here to stay," he told his audience. "The architect must use this normal tool of civilization to best advantage." He did not, he said, believe in teamwork products. It was the individual who gave a work its art.

This speech, widely circulated, and the houses Wright had built, brought many clients. He transferred his office to his Oak Park home and added a wing that included a study, library, reception room, and skylighted drafting room large enough to accomodate apprentices.

Wright worked very hard, but occasionally he and Catherine went to dances, the theater, or concerts. With the children, who numbered six after the births of Catherine, David, Frances, and Llewelyn, Wright was gay and imaginative. At the back of the second floor of their home he designed a barrel-ceilinged playroom that had fanciful chandeliers and a scene from *Arabian Nights* over the fireplace. Evenings the family read aloud and made music together, with each child joining the family orchestra as soon as he was old enough. Sometimes the Wrights traveled to the Lloyd-Jones farms in Wisconsin, where they hiked, rode horseback, and went on picnics.

41 □

But commissions coming in for public buildings as well as houses whittled away time for family fun. A spare but beautiful building designed for the Larkin Company in Buffalo, New York, was one of the first to have metal-bound plate-glass doors and windows, metal furniture, and air conditioning. Inside the building a four-story well was topped by a huge skylight and surrounded by galleries of office space. Pictures of the steel-structured cliff of brick with staircase towers that pushed out from the corners were published around the world.

After completion of the Larkin Building, Wright turned to the Unity Temple for Oak Park. As he wrestled at night with problems of a building to be used for education and recreation as well as for worship, he would be encouraged by Catherine's piano playing.

His design for a flat-roofed, H-shaped structure with no spire would have been rejected had he not argued persuasively with the help of a drawn-to-scale model. This marked the first time poured concrete was used in a monumental public edifice. Blocks had been processed to give the appearance of marble. Balconies projected from walls into central spaces. Congratulations poured in after the first service in the Temple auditorium that had geometric ornament and a skylight much like a giant egg crate.

Most of the residences Wright built during this period were in cities, but he thought that the prairies around them called for homes that had sheltering roofs and hugged the earth. Frequently they had windows that were continuous ribbons of glass. Interior spaces were open to one another and to the outdoors. At the heart of every house there was a broad fireplace, often of rock. Always there were visual surprises—a high ceiling after a low one or an unexpected glimpse of the landscape. These houses came to be known as prairie houses.

One of the finest of these was a complex of buildings of stucco and ornamental tile designed for Mr. and Mrs. Avery Coonley at Riverside, Illinois. The living room, with its fern motif echoed by a mural on the wall and with metal grille windows, had an air of palatial luxury.

Conservatives objected to omission of attics, basements, and fancy porches in the prairie houses. Contractors, puzzled by absence of traditional features, sometimes failed to read blueprints correctly. Bankers often refused to finance them.

However, Wright's work was given a special room at the Chicago Architecture Club. *The Ladies' Home Journal* commissioned him to design a prairie house for its readers, and *Architectural Record* called the Robie House, in Chicago, one of the seven most notable residences ever built in America. Constructed of tawny brick and stone with roof of red tile and eaves of copper, this house had long deck-like balconies and superb masonry.

Wright was earning good commissions, but expenses spiraled as the children grew older and he provided them with bicycles and horses. He wanted fine clothes for Catherine and himself and liked to fill the house with beautiful things—fresh-cut flowers, paintings, the glint of silver. Catherine was as extravagant as he was, and there was never enough money to pay their bills.

Harried by debts and keyed up about building projects, Wright would be too tired to sleep. Lack of rest made him supersensitive to the shouts, quarrels, and drumbeats of the children, and he was often short-tempered. He and Catherine, who had never been able to understand his dedication to his work, drifted apart. Frank argued that it might be best to break off a marriage in which aims were no longer mutual, but Catherine opposed a divorce.

Wright was equally discouraged about his career. He failed to get several important commissions he very much wanted. Buildings that had been completed drew criticism from those loyal to old forms of architecture.

At about that time he had a letter from Ernst Wasmuth, a Berlin publisher of art works. Wasmuth hoped to publish a portfolio of Wright's buildings. He wanted Wright to come to edit it.

A period of voluntary exile in Europe might solve some of his problems, thought Frank. To get money for the trip and to provide for his family in his absence, he sold some valuable Japanese prints, collected funds due from clients, and turned current projects over to Chicago architect Herman von Holst.

Publication of the Wasmuth portfolio made Wright a hero among young architects in Europe. But when he returned to the United States, newspapers attacked and reviled him for desertion of his family. Nothing had changed at home, and he and Catherine agreed to live apart.

Wright built a home on rocky, wooded land his mother gave him on a hill near Spring Green, Wisconsin. The house of native stone and wood hugged the hillside. The low-slung pitched roof had a deep overhang. In one wing there was a studio and a drafting room.

Wright called his home Taliesin—Welsh for "shining brow." His mother, his children, and other guests visited frequently. Apprentices came to work there, but Wright shuttled back and forth between Taliesin and Chicago, where he still had an office.

In 1913 he got the commission for Midway Gardens—a recreational center to include a spacious central court, casino, a large restaurant, and a concert hall. His son John, who had settled on architecture as a career and had high purpose and sensitivity, assisted him. Together they planned a complex of buildings with towers, trellises, and striking ornamentation.

Frank and John were eating lunch at the almost completed Midway Gardens on the Fourth of July, 1914, when word came that there was a fire at Taliesin. By the time Wright reached home, flames and smoke had ruined the building except for the studio wing. But what grieved him most was the loss of life. A servant had gone mad, set fire to the house, and then killed one of Wright's apprentices, three workmen, a woman who had become a close friend of Wright's, and her two children.

Friends wanted Wright to leave Taliesin, but he insisted on staying on in the studio. For weeks he could not free himself from loneliness, despair, and anguish. But gradually his courage returned. On the ashes of the old house he built a new one much like the first, except that he added a wing for his mother and his aunts Nell and Jane.

A flattering and challenging commission came his way when he was invited to build the Imperial Hotel in Tokyo just outside the grounds of the Emperor's palace. The hotel presented unusual problems because the site was a cheeselike soil that overlay liquid and the structure must be guaranteed to be quake-proof.

After much research on the effects of earthquakes on buildings, Wright hit upon floating the hotel on a foundation of mud so it would rock with quakes instead of resisting them. To his son John, who had joined him, he explained his plans for cantilevered floors with projecting beams or girders fixed at one end to a rigid support. Division of the building into small parts that would move independently of one another would give protection against earth tremors.

But new problems kept popping up. Wright found it hard to get his ideas across to engineers and workmen who spoke a different language and wanted to use their hands instead of machines. The rainy season interfered with construction. At one time the whole project was threatened because the board of directors thought he was spending too much money. Baron Okura, who had become a staunch friend, shamed the directors into support.

In the hours that he was away from the drafting board or the construction site, Wright read, played the piano, or rambled around the country ferreting out fine prints to buy. As he traveled he stored up ideas to take with him—the use of heating elements underneath floors, the way native builders revealed or heightened the contours of grained wood. Wright also became much interested in the Shinto philosophy of clean hands, clean heart, clean purposes.

During the six years Wright was supervising the Imperial Hotel he returned at intervals to the United States, working out of a Los Angeles office. For Aline Barnsdall, who had a deep interest in drama, he designed impressive Hollyhock House, so called because the flower was a motif in the ornament.

Back in Japan, Wright became ill from the combined effects of the climate and excessive work and strain. His mother, although over eighty, came to care for him. While she was there the Emperor gave a garden party in her honor.

The Imperial Hotel when finally completed was really an aggregate of buildings. The exterior of greenish-yellow lava and gold-colored brick blended with copper gave a luxurious effect. Terraces, courts, pools, and connecting bridges lent variety. The Imperial Household conferred upon Wright the title of Kenchiko Ho, "High Builder." On the day he left Japan, workmen crowded around his car shouting affectionate farewells.

In the United States the *Architectural Record* cited the Imperial as "The high-water mark thus far attained by a modern architect." Its engineering was as sound as its artistry. During a quake in 1923 that left much of Tokyo in ruins, the undamaged hotel became a shelter for the homeless.

For a time after his return from Japan, Wright practiced architecture in California. Lloyd, who had also followed his father's profession, assisted him. Wright had always sought ways to add beauty to native materials that would be suitable to terrain and climate. Now he developed a new method of using concrete blocks, strengthened by being threaded with metal reinforcements and then filled with poured concrete. One of the most outstanding of a series of houses employing this system was La Miniatura built for Mrs. Alice Millard in Pasadena. The balconied building with ornamentally patterned concrete brick stood tall and lovely between two eucalyptus trees.

Homesick for Taliesin, Wright gave up his California office and went back to Wisconsin. But his personal life was complicated and

Imperial Hotel, Tokyo, Japan, by Frank Lloyd Wright. Photograph by Palmer Pictures.

unhappy. His mother and other close relatives died. Taliesin was again destroyed by fire, and his second marriage was a failure. After Catherine had finally granted him a divorce, Wright had married sculptress Miriam Noel, a striking, sophisticated woman. Miriam had always suffered from emotional disturbances, but at Taliesin her mental and physical health declined alarmingly. After she left Wright and Taliesin she supplied reporters with lurid stories about him, portraying him as an eccentric, immoral man. Even after the divorce the harrassment continued.

During this same period, Wright had more than his share of office tragedies. He spent months designing and working at the Arizona site of a three-hundred-room winter resort hotel. A national depression stopped construction. Instead of the forty thousand dollars he had been promised, Wright was in debt nineteen thousand dollars for the Ocatilla work camp set up to accommodate his apprentices.

The depression also brought cancellation of his design for a nineteen-story apartment house and office building in New York. While commissions declined, debts piled up. Wright had still owed money on Taliesin II when it burned. To this was added the expense of rebuilding and maintaining Taliesin III. From Japan he had brought back dozens of prints for individuals and for museums. A number of these turned out to be fraudulent reproductions. Wright felt obligated to replace them, although it cost him thirty thousand dollars. All these expenses, plus alimony to Miriam and salaries to apprentices, exhausted his resources. Creditors became impatient and finally took possession of Taliesin III.

During these dark days, Wright never went completely down under the struggle, humiliation, and suffering because he still was driven by great ideals. In pressing toward his architectural goals he had the encouragement of a new friend who made him aware of his assets—genius, courage, energy.

As soon as he had been introduced to divorcée Olgivanna

Lazovich, he had sensed a strength in her like the strength of fine metal. Member of an aristocratic family of Montenegro, Olgivanna was handsome, artistic, and intelligent. After she consented to marry him, Frank felt as if he could handle anything the future might bring. He had already grown very fond of Olgivanna's appealing seven-year-old daughter Svetlana, and having a family again gave him security. He was further encouraged by the action of friends who believed in his talents so strongly that they gave him enough financial assistance to repossess Taliesin.

But Wright got very few chances to build—partly because of paralyzing depression, partly because of unfavorable publicity. His architecture was daring and critics called it crack-brained, impractical, expensive. Lectures, articles he wrote, royalties on his books *An Autobiography* and *The Disappearing City* brought occasional checks. But there were times when getting funds for even the next meal seemed a problem.

One day, Wright stood viewing the idle, neglected buildings of the Hillside Home School that he had designed some years ago for his aunts who had operated the school. It struck him that they would provide an ideal dormitory. Why not set up a school in which young would-be architects could learn the nature and uses of materials and have actual experiences in building?

Wright had already proved in lectures at various universities that he could capture the enthusiasm of students. When he had gone to São Paulo, Brazil, as a member of a jury to judge drawings submitted in a worldwide competition for a memorial to Columbus, students of the Brazilian Belles Artes had followed him in droves.

As he described to Olgivanna his plan for a Fellowship, Frank confided that he could not teach architecture, because it was something one had to experience, but he could teach principles. She encouraged him to go ahead and helped him write and sent out circulars describing accomodations and aims of the Fellowship.

On October 1, 1923, Wright met with twenty-three apprentices ready to begin their training. There would be no formal lectures and no system of examinations, grades, or diplomas, he told his students. The only test would be their competence in building. There were a few principles, he said, that would be adhered to, but beyond that the young architects should draw on their own individuality. At first, partly because he waived tuition for needy students, Wright had trouble making ends meet. Olgivanna, who cooked or did anything that was needed, had to serve boiled turnips frequently. When the temperature fell much below zero, the generator froze and there were no lights. A few of the students turned out to be lazy, hot-tempered, incompetent, or ill-suited to group living. Those who could not learn to do better were weeded out. But the response of talented, able students convinced Wright that the Fellowship would be a success.

During the spring and summer months, apprentices worked outdoors building but also gardening, chopping trees, performing farm chores and tasks connected with the cooperative life at Taliesin. Architects, said Wright, must be strong in body and character.

Because part of that strength could be gained through wholesome recreation, he provided weekly picnics, berry or nut picking, boat parties on the pond in summer, ice skating in winter. Evenings, apprentices and the wives of married ones got together to stage amateur theatricals, see good movies, or make music. Apprentices always sang with gusto the "T Square and Triangle" song Wright had composed.

Sunday night everyone dressed up and had dinner on trays in the art-filled living room at Taliesin. Afterward they talked about everything from books to life. Distinguished visitors often shared the exalted conversation.

"Young fellows," Wright said one night, "need a desire, a feeling that they want the best, the highest, and truest." Such goals, he cautioned, required sacrifice and would not be reached through soft living.

During these informal discussions and also in the drafting room, Wright often touched on the evils of urbanization. He loved the vigor of cities but hated their ugliness and artificiality.

"Cities, as we know them," he told his apprentices, "force men into an unnatural way of life."

To make tangible to students his ideas of what cities should be like, Wright launched a project he called "Broadacre City," a self-contained community. On a large relief map, apprentices made built-to-scale models of houses, farms, factories. There were a few apartment houses, but the bulk of the population lived in houses close to fields and flowers. Home owners had an acre of land apiece.

Wright gave much time to the Broadacre project and to the Fellowship, but he never let it rob him of time with his family that now included little Iovanna. The whole family had horses and liked to ride. Nights they often read together.

During the late thirties, Wright's architectural practice began to revive, but instead of disbanding the Fellowship he expanded it and let apprentices work alongside him at construction sites.

"Beware of shortcuts," he cautioned. "No detail is too small to merit painstaking attention. Shoddy materials, inferior workmanship betray the client but also betray yourself.

To apprentices who worked with Wright at Bear Run, Pennsylvania, where he built a house for Edgar Kaufmann, Wright gave a lesson in the dramatic use of rock and water. The steel, concrete, and glass house rested on a rocky ledge. Cantilevered porches extended out over a waterfall and seemed to float in space. The "Falling Water" House in all its wild romantic beauty became one of the best-known residences in the world.

Wright liked building palatial houses, but he believed America's major architectural problem was building moderately priced houses that would have originality and artistic excellence. Because he visualized these dwellings as suitable for an ideal democratic America he called them Usonian, a term derived from United

States of North America. A house for Herbert Jacobs at Westmoreland, near Madison, became a kind of pilot project for these low-cost homes. Other Usonian homes were built in many parts of the country. All had simplicity and dignity, and some achieved an appearance of elegance.

Industrial buildings as well as houses enhanced Wright's reputation. While designing the S. C. Johnson and Son Administration Building for Racine, Wisconsin, he worked with the idea of making it a home away from home for employees. In the plans he included squash courts and a small auditorium that could be used for lectures or movies. The streamlined exterior of the brick walls was broken only by horizontal bands of glass tubing.

Wright had introduced many innovations such as the use of graceful concrete columns with cores of steel mesh to support the ceiling of the interior office space. At the time of the formal opening of the Johnson Building, an interviewer asked him for comment. "I like the building," he said. "They like it. Let it go at that."

Magazines, newspapers, radio had much more to say; in 1938, *Architectural Forum* devoted an entire issue to Wright's work.

Wright was too involved in new projects to pay much attention to the publicity. Severe Wisconsin winters that halted building and kept the Fellowship busy hauling wood for fireplaces persuaded him to transfer his headquarters to Arizona during the coldest months of the year. After several winters at a temporary tent camp, Wright purchased a site in Paradise Valley near Phoenix.

For Taliesin West, he designed buildings with massive walls of desert concrete—gold, green, and quartz stones, gathered by the apprentices and bound together by concrete. Rich and bold in form, the buildings had a dramatic silhouette but gave a feeling of oneness with cacti and barren rock. Deeply cantilevered roof rafters were topped by canvas. Apprentices lived in tent houses with waist-high rock walls and canvas roofs.

On the desert, Wright conducted the Fellowship along much

"Falling Water" House, Bear Run, Pennsylvania, by Frank Lloyd Wright. Photograph by Wayne Andrews.

the same lines as in Wisconsin, with practice in designing and building. He also continued long give-and-take conversations with students. Freedom was a favorite theme, but freedom without conscience, he said, is dangerous.

"You have to be wholeheartedly into anything in order to achieve what is worth having," he told apprentices. "If your allegiance is divided, if your thought is divided, if your feeling is confused, get rid of that condition. To have a cause and a loyalty to it makes a man."

During the summers when Wright and the Fellowship returned to Wisconsin, Olgivanna's brother Vlado and his wife Sophie watched over Taliesin West.

In 1939, Solomon R. Guggenheim, industrialist, philanthropist, patron of arts and music, asked Wright to design a museum to house contemporary art, Wright evolved a plan for a building in which visitors would take an elevator to the top floor and then walk down three-quarters of a mile of continuous, curving ramp with paintings displayed along the side. After Guggenheim examined the design, he turned to Wright and exclaimed, "That is it! This is what I wanted. You are the only man who could have done it."

Construction was postponed because of high building costs, but other activities filled Wright's time. At the invitation of the Royal Institute of Architects and London University he went to England to give a series of lectures. With him he took Olgivanna and twelve-year-old Iovanna.

In his lectures, Wright appealed to architects to become poets and interpreters of their times. "Science," he said, "gives the tools in the box but cannot save us. Architects must make humane use of these tools." While he was in England, the Royal Institute conferred upon him the Royal Gold Medal.

The days abroad made Wright acutely aware of the tension and unrest being created by Hitler in Europe. War seemed inevitable, he told his friends when he returned to America. It erupted the following September. Construction almost ground to a halt, but Wright was able to complete several Usonian houses and a moderately priced apartment house called Suntop Homes at Ardmore, Pennsylvania.

He also began designing the entire campus of Florida Southern College in Lakewood. As always while he sketched, he was filled with anticipation. Yet at intervals he wrestled with doubts and a little fear. He discarded one design after another; small scale drawings came first, then larger ones.

Final plans called for steel-reinforced concrete buildings connected by deeply shaded esplanades. The Ann Pfeiffer Chapel, a white concrete building with strong horizontal lines, had a tower and wall perforations filled with cut glass. The war slowed the pace of construction.

During these years of conflict, Wright's thoughts were on preservation of democracy as much as on architecture, but by democracy he did not mean a political system alone. True democracy, he believed, could be achieved only by discipline from within.

To give circulation to some of his views he wrote *When Democracy Builds*. In this book he appealed to readers to make a more honest, more inspiring world. Wright's works and words were becoming known in many lands. He was deeply touched when in the midst of England's struggle for survival, King George VI honored him with the award of His Majesty's Royal Medal.

After the war, Wright, caught up in the building boom, often worked ten or more hours a day designing houses, a hotel, a laundry. He continued work on the Florida Southern campus and built an unconventional gift shop for V. C. Morris in San Francisco. The façade was a blank wall of buff-colored brick. For the interior, Wright created poetic loveliness with a spiral ramp that curved up gracefully toward a huge circular glass dome. Glass, silver, and china were displayed in walnut cabinets and shelves.

Concurrently with the store, Wright had under construction a

Unitarian church in Madison. Walls were of native limestone. The trussed roof with copper had a steep upthrust that resembled hands clasped in prayer.

Meanwhile the construction of houses had gone forward in many parts of the country. No two were alike. A house for toymaker Sol Friedman near Pleasantville, New York, had two interesting circles, but a house for Professor Paul Hanna at Palo Alto was hexagonal. At Libertyville, Illinois, he put a house on stilts to give the Lloyd Lewis family a view of the Des Plaines River. For some of these houses he designed built-in furniture.

A home he particularly enjoyed designing was for his son David on the Arizona desert. Raised on concrete piers, it resembled a flattened snail in shape. Circular roofs were enameled a coppery blue-green. Guests entered the house by a long ramp bordered with flowers. Wright also planned his son Llewelyn's home at Bethesda, Maryland. Built of stone block, glass, and Philippine mahogany, it grew out of the ground on a mushroomlike base of poured concrete.

Because he sometimes underestimated costs or changed his mind on materials to be used, Wright gave a few of his clients harrowing experiences. But the resultant homes usually had a plus something. All had a few common characteristics—they linked indoors and outdoors, blending with their surroundings whether woods, waterfalls, or sand. And in his use of building materials he showed respect for their inherent characteristics.

In 1949, Wright went to Houston, Texas, to receive the Gold Medal awarded by the American Institute of Architects in recognition of most distinguished service to the architectural profession. Other important awards followed.

Wright's utterances were widely circulated. The press often mistook statements made half in fun and quoted him seriously. Of Washington, D.C., he said, "The whole place looks like a stone quarry gone out of business." He referred to Los Angeles as "a group of suburbs in search of a city."

He reserved his most pointed barbs for members of his own profession. What was wrong with architecture, he said, was the architects. He had little but contempt for International Style architecture, so called because its practitioners believed in use of modern techniques international in character. Products of this school, Wright insisted, were mere boxes with steel bones and flat faces.

Wright's outspoken style and assumed arrogance had made him unpopular among professional architects in the past. But at architectural meetings in the fifties, no one any longer challenged him even though he made outrageous statements. His personality was so commanding that when he entered a room of fellow architects they almost involuntarily got to their feet.

But his caustic wit did sometimes cost him commissions, and so did his liberalism. On a trip to Russia he had been given a royal welcome and later, misled by intellectuals, he had leaned to the Left. He soon discovered that his democratic beliefs clashed with those of the communists and he had nothing more to do with them, but the government bypassed him when selecting architects for public buildings.

However, Wright had more commissions than he could handle. When the Johnson company asked him to add a Laboratory Tower to the original building, the structure of a tree gave him the idea for his design. The central core of the tower, much like a tree trunk, contained elevators, ducts, wires, and pipes for essential services. Floors were cantilevered from a central steel mast anchored to a concrete foundation that penetrated over fifty feet into the ground. On the exterior, salmon-colored brick alternated with glass water-green tubing.

Asked for his comment on the building, Wright said, "It is a sample of the conversion of a rampant industrial system from weed into flower."

Wright again made use of cross-shaped spine and cantilevered floors in the Price Tower in Bartlesville, Oklahoma. Areas of glass, soft-toned concrete, and parapets faced with blue-green copper gave a constant interplay of colors. Tinted glass and copper blades shaded offices and dwelling sectors from drafts and too much sunshine. The soaring tower is visible from sixteen miles away.

During the same period, the Fellowship expanded. Apprentices now came from all over the world, staying various lengths of time from two hours to twenty years. Apprentice Wesley Peters had come to Taliesin in the 1930's and fallen in love with Svetlana. After their marriage they had left Taliesin for a time but then had moved back. Svetlana's artistic and musical talent and Wesley's alertness, energy, and architectural know-how had given much to the Fellowship.

With the help of his apprentices, Wright continued to make improvements at both Taliesins. The Wisconsin site became a self-contained world with farm buildings, guest rooms, laundry, a theater, shops, and studios for printing, painting, weaving, pottery, machine and model making. At Taliesin West, Wright surrounded the buildings with bamboo and oleander trees, gardens of desert flowers, a play court, and pools. The living room with masses of stone was linked to the outdoors by a garden room with glass panels facing cacti, shrubs, and flowers. The theater was enlarged.

Certain traditions grew up at each of the Taliesins. In Wisconsin apprentices always celebrated Wright's June eighth birthday. And there was an end-of-summer festival. All the apprentices could sing, dance, or play a musical instrument, and festivals were planned around a theme carried out with the help of costumes, dramatics, decorations, and music. At Taliesin West, Iovanna and Olgivanna directed an annual Festival of Music and Dance.

Wright could communicate with his apprentices at a festival or in the drafting room because he retained his energy, optimism, and belief in the future. He became very fond of his students, and after they left Taliesin he followed their careers with interest.

Letters from apprentices, added to those from clients, friends, the public, and aspiring architects, made correspondence a burden.

S. C. Johnson and Son Administration Building in Racine, Wisconsin, by Frank Lloyd Wright. Photograph courtesy S. C. Johnson and Son, Inc.

Olgivanna or a secretary helped, but Wright frequently answered the letters himself. When a child wrote and asked if he would draw a plan for a doghouse, he sent a design for one.

Many of the letters were invitations to speak. Whether talking to students on a campus, to a woman's club, or to a group of artists, Wright was forceful and original. He had both the appearance and talents of an actor and was much in demand for television appearances. His talks were punctuated by humor, but his messages were usually serious ones.

"I do not deny the value of reason," he said on one occasion, "but we should in no way allow the poetry of life, the beauty and inspiration of our divinity, to be submerged by reasoning power." To students, he said, "Wisdom is not created by man; it must come to him . . . . It comes to those whose minds are pure and whose hearts are open to receive it. Intellect must be illumined by love."

Architects, he said, must strive to give service, not to win profit or fame. A building, he insisted, expressed the qualities of the builder. A flashy, dishonest architect produced that kind of building.

To deliver speeches, to oversee projects under way, to confer with clients, to receive awards, Wright had to travel a great deal, both in the United States and abroad. Olgivanna went with him. In Venice, Wright accepted the Italian Star of Solidarity and in the city of Florence, Italy, where he received the De Medici Medal, adolescents followed him begging for autographs. Many foreign universities bestowed honorary degrees; organizations such as the Akademie der Kunst in Berlin made Wright an honorary member. Architectural societies in Mexico, Finland, and other countries offered honorary membership.

At home, also, Wright was granted numerous honorary degrees and elected to membership in distinguished organizations. The American Academy of Arts and Letters awarded him a gold medal. He received the Peter Cooper Award for Advancement of Art.

When *Time* magazine polled five hundred architects, asking

them to name the Seven Wonders of American architecture, Wright received three of the nominations for his Robie House, Johnson Wax Building, and Falling Water House. The November 1955 issue of *House Beautiful* was devoted to pictures of Wright's work, interviews, and articles about him.

One of the tributes that pleased him most was a banquet given in Madison in 1955 to show him how Wisconsonians honored his work. He was overwhelmed by the standing ovation and a check for ten thousand dollars. Various groups exhibited his work in cities around the world. One of the most elaborate was one sponsored by the Guggenheim Foundation titled "Sixty Years of Living Architecture." Besides hundreds of drawings, photo murals, and plates, it included a life-size mock-up of a house. The purpose was to show how modern homes use principles borrowed from Wright, such as horizontal lines and a close relationship between indoors and out-doors.

During the period of honors, exhibits, and awards, Wright was designing a variety of structures. He was constantly on the lookout for new uses of materials, new techniques of expression. These won acclaim but there were reverses, too. Some projects remained only on paper. A towerlike hotel in Dallas remained unbuilt because of the death of the client. When King Feisal II of Iraq asked Wright to design an opera house and auditorium, he evolved a plan that would have been very elegant. The project came to an end when revolutionaries murdered the king.

Sometimes Wright used his designs in a fantastic way to make a point. For Chicago's lake front he drew a mile-high, needle-shaped tower that would accommodate 150,000 employees. Had it ever been built, to move people, supplies, and services it would have been necessary to raze the center of Chicago. This is what he had in mind.

During the 1950's Wright had underway many buildings other than mile-high ones. These included the Guggenheim Museum. Solomon Guggenheim had died in 1949, but his nephew Harry

61 □

Guggenheim, president of the board of trustees, had decided to go ahead with the original plans.

To build the museum took years of endless conferences and revisions. Wright wanted walls of white cement and crushed white marble that would slope gently outward to form a giant spiral. Light for exhibits would be provided by a skylight dome and strips of glass above spiraling walls. Paintings would be viewed from ramps flowing from floor to floor.

While the Guggenheim progressed, Wright was working on the Kalita Humphreys Memorial Theater in Dallas, a Byzantine Greek Church in Milwaukee, Beth Sholom Synagogue near Philadelphia, and projects elsewhere. Because Frank had to spend much of his time in the East, he and Olgivanna rented a suite of rooms at the Plaza Hotel in New York. They completely redesigned it. Wall panels of Japanese gold paper and red velvet curtains set off tables, easels, and chairs done in black lacquer with red edges. To the suite came many visitors and friends. One of Wright's favorites was the prominent architect Edward D. Stone.

For years Wright had given many hours to writing. Among published books had been *An Organic Architecture* and *Genius and Mobocracy*. Now, in the apartment at the Plaza, he and Olga, who also wrote, turned out more articles and books. In *The Living City* he wrote, "Our soul grows more by what we give than what we take and feed upon." Wright's philosophy was more fully expressed in *A Testament*. "Success in architecture," he said, took "depth of character and dedication to principle, to beauty, and to nature's ways."

By November, 1958, the Guggenheim Museum was almost finished. As he and Olga stood before it Wright was exhilarated. He had heard criticisms of it. Someone had even said that Wright hated modern art and so had built this museum to destroy it. But he saw the wholeness of the building that had emerged after so many struggles. For him it was a symbol of freedom and of beauty. Workmen coming out of the museum looked at him silently, respectfully.

□ 62

An architectural student stopped and asked him to pose for a picture.

Back home in Taliesin West, Wright busied himself writing, speaking, and planning the Grady Gammage Auditorium and Music Building for Arizona State University. He also gave many hours to Fellowship activities. During one of the evening discussion periods he told his apprentices, "You are the shape hewers and knowers. This takes strength of mind and muscles, but also strength of character and heart."

Early in 1959, Wright's mind often turned to the Guggenheim. The grand opening was to include a preview, a dinner, and a reception. Mayor Wagner would be there, as would state and federal officials. President Eisenhower had sent a letter to be read at the ceremonies. As Easter drew near, Wright, among other projects, was planning an enclosed garden for Taliesin East that would give Olgivanna seclusion.

But he put all his drawings aside to enter into plans for the annual festival. On Easter morning he listened to the Fellowship chorus and then watched the children hunt for eggs. There was the usual outdoor breakfast and later a movie on the life of Jesus. His enjoyment of the festival was heightened because among the special guests were his daughter Catherine, and his sons David and Lloyd and their families.

That night as he listened to a friend play Beethoven, Frank looked at Olgivanna, who had been beside him throughout the day. They had shared innumerable happy days, he thought, but this was the happiest of all.

A few days later, on April 4, Wright was stricken with severe pain while he was at his drawing board. Olga rushed him to a hospital in Phoenix. He died April 9, 1959.

Many mourned the loss of the man believed by some to have been the greatest architect of the twentieth century. But nothing can destroy an idea, and Wright had given the world many ideas. Because he used materials expertly and avoided shoddiness, his buildings were solid and substantial, but they also had dignity and individuality. These qualities were recognized when the United States Department of the Interior made the Robie House a national historic landmark. Through his singleness of purpose, his persistence, and his attitude toward work as an adventure, Wright achieved a record unmatched in architectural history.

But he was an uncommon man as well as an uncommon architect. People said he was arrogant, egotistical, intolerant. On the surface he sometimes was, but his was a quest for the bravest and best, and friends found him understanding and generous.

Frank Lloyd Wright always had the courage to take the hard path. A less brave man would have gone down in defeat when confronted by financial setbacks, a twice-destroyed Taliesin, last-minute cancellations of building projects, personal entanglements. The way he faced up to stark tragedy, the beauty of the vision he held for his life and his world, moved men's minds and kindled their hearts.

THREE

WALTER GROPIUS

Builder and Teacher

Walter Gropius, while still a student, designed and helped to build a group of workmen's houses on his Uncle Erich's estate in Pomerania. This activity appealed to him more than classroom lectures at the Berlin Technische Hochschule, although he was a brilliant student. A one-year period of compulsory military service had taken Walter away from the Institute of Technology in Munich. Now his classes at the Berlin school were interrupted when he inherited a thousand marks willed to him by an aunt. He could finish his education through travel, he told his family.

Walter visited England and Italy. In Spain, in 1907, he observed buildings but also studied ceramics, worked in a pottery factory, and did odd jobs. Always he had an eye to getting experiences that would make him a better architect. While Walter was in Spain, his father wrote that craftsmanship had become a Gropius tradition. In the family there had been teachers, clergymen, government officials, but all had artistic tendencies. Mr. Gropius himself, privy surveyor for the city of Berlin, had a strong interest in painting and in art publications.

Another Gropius characteristic was love of nature, thought Walter, as he reread his father's letter. During most of his childhood the family had lived in an apartment in Berlin, where Mrs. Gropius was a charming hostess to the many visitors. But whenever possible, the family had retreated to the country. Very often, Walter had gone alone to the estates of two uncles in Pomerania and Posen where he roamed at will.

At the end of a year in Spain, Walter, now twenty-four, had had enough of travel and of ceramics. Back in Berlin he became an apprentice in the office of Peter Behrens, a much publicized architect who served as design consultant to a leading German electrical trust, the A.E.G.

Gropius was disappointed when Behrens set him to work designing light fixtures, but he exerted himself to produce original products. He had to compete with other highly talented assistants, but he showed such promise that Behrens made him his chief assistant. In this post he had exposure to the whole range of design problems, from factories and office buildings down to manufactured products.

For Walter's twenty-seventh birthday, on May 18, 1910, the talented draftsman Mies van der Rohe, the young Swiss-born architect Le Corbusier, and other friends gave a party. It was in the back room of a cheap restaurant, but the setting did not matter. He had never spent a happier evening, Gropius told his friends.

Gropius liked his work and his companions in Behrens' office, but he wanted to practice on his own. For months he searched newspapers and periodicals for announcements of projected buildings in Berlin and elsewhere. Whenever he saw one he offered his services to its sponsors. He got only rejections. But finally in 1910 the indus-

Walter Gropius

trialist Bensheid asked him to submit a design for a shoe factory to be built at Alfeld and to be called the Fagus factory.

For years Gropius had been preparing for this opportunity. He envisioned a building that would use glass, concrete, and steel instead of the brick that had so long been considered a standard item. And he wanted a building that would get away from dead styles and fussy ornamentation. He sketched a three-story factory with a glass curtain wall—glass and metal hung outside the columns and outside the skeleton of steel. By moving the corner column back from its historic location and cantilevering the unsupported floor slab, he could enclose the corner with a glass screen.

Gropius was elated when the Fagus board accepted a design most industrialists would have considered radical. The completed building had a skeletal lightness and grace. With one leap Gropius had sprung into architectural maturity. His family expressed their pride, but his mother disapproved of the comment of the press that he was "modern." It was like tying a label around a bottle, she said, to call his style thus and so. Anyway, she was concerned, she told him, not about the building but about the man behind the tag.

Success had not gone to his head, Gropius assured her; he still had much to learn. He had plenty of opportunity to do so. The Fagus Building led to commissions for other factories and for residences. All were distinguished by clean lines, use of unusual materials, and absence of ornamentation. Gropius also designed luxury furniture for a villa, steel furniture for a battleship, and a sleeping car for the German railways. For designs submitted in a world exhibition in Ghent he received a gold medal.

Even when away from his drawing board, Gropius' mind centered on architecture. He was an active member of the Architekten Verein and the Deutscher Werkbund, the latter being an association of artists, workmen, and industrialists dedicated to the goal of cooperation between art and industry and improvement of the quality and workmanship of products. He contributed articles to the yearbook of the Werkbund and designed a model factory for their exhibit in Cologne in 1914. To get materials to build it, Gropius traveled throughout Germany getting promises of bricks from one factory, glass from another, and money from others. His three-part building with administrative offices, garage, and factory areas had some faults but it attracted worldwide attention to the idea of better designs for industrial buildings.

Before the exhibition was scheduled to close, rumors came of possibility of war between Austria and Serbia. Before the war had become a reality, Gropius had a summons to join the armed forces.

During the conflict, he had some terrifying experiences. Once when he was sent out in a plane to make observations, the plane was shot down. Another time in an area under attack he lay for hours buried under rubble and corpses. After his rescue, ambulance aides took him to a field hospital to recover from shock and wounds.

While he was there a letter came from Alma Mahler, whom he had met at a spa in Toblach, Switzerland, several years before. Since then, her husband, the distinguished conductor and composer Gustav Mahler, had died. She was now alone except for her daughter Anna, nicknamed Gucki.

Alma wrote that she had heard of his brilliant showing at the Cologne Exhibition, terminated by the war. She wanted to congratulate him on his achievements. This set off an exchange of letters. In February, 1915, while Gropius was in Berlin on convalescent leave, Alma came to see him. During the next two weeks they fell in love.

They were married the following August, but Gropius had to return to the front and had only short leaves after that. Over a year later, word came that Walter was a father. Alma and he named the baby girl Manon.

Once during the war the Grand Duke of Saxe-Weimar summoned Gropius to come immediately for an interview. "Would you?" the Duke asked, "take over the Grand Ducal school of arts and crafts in Weimar after the war is ended?"

Gropius fingered the fur cap which was part of his Hussar's uniform. Teaching, he thought, would appeal to him, but the school had been headed by the great Belgian architect Henry van de Velde, who had been discharged only because his native land was now an enemy of Germany. How could he hope to measure up to the performance of this gifted man? He consented only after the Duke told him that Van de Velde himself had recommended Gropius.

Back at the front, Gropius devised new techniques for signaling, but his thoughts were often on his family and postwar plans. Alma's letters worried him. At first she had written that she wanted nothing more than to make him happy. But lately she had sounded ecstatic over the poems of Franz Werfel.

By the end of the war, Gropius had earned the right of a hero's welcome, having been awarded both the Second and First Class Iron Cross, the Bavarian Military Medal for Merit, the Austrian

Royal Decoration for Military Merit, and a Mark of Distinction for wounds.

Everything would be different now, he thought jubilantly, as he sped toward his waiting family.

At home, joy turned to desolation when Alma told him that although he had been loyal and generous she had fallen in love with the poet Franz Werfel. Gropius regained hope after she promised to try to save their marriage. He plunged into plans for the school he was to head. The Duke of Weimar followed his suggestion for a merger of the Academy of Art, a branch of the Weimar school system, with the school of arts and crafts under the name of the Bauhaus or "House of Building."

At the Bauhaus, Gropius hoped to find a way to bridge the gap between the arts and also to unite art and industrial products. He believed that machinery had become the modern medium of design and thought architects must come to terms with it. But he saw no reason why artistic values had to be sacrificed to mass production.

On the cover of the four-page program Gropius offered to prospective students appeared the slogan, "Together We Desire, We Design, and We Create the New Building in which Architecture, Painting, and Sculpture are One Complete Unity."

When he went to Weimar in the spring of 1919 to open the Bauhaus, his wife, Gucki, and Manon went with him. But Alma and he differed in their interests and values. Reluctantly Walter consented to a divorce.

Gropius tried to ease the loneliness after loss of his family by immersing himself in Bauhaus affairs. Although he was a born teacher and organizer, it was not easy to launch a school with young men who ranged widely in age and abilities.

Some of the students, victims of the chaos and poverty that stalked Germany, arrived barefoot, wearing remnants of military uniforms. All were accepted for a trial period. All took a six-month

Bauhaus, Dessau, Germany, by Walter Gropius. Photograph courtesy The Museum of Modern Art.

preliminary course. In this course, Gropius introduced students to proportion, scale, and color, and to machines and materials used in mass production.

After completion of the preliminary course, the student entered a workshop of his own choice—ceramics, carpentry, furniture design, metals, weaving, or painting. The aim was not only to teach students to use their hands but to guide them to an understanding of the tools of the machine age. Gropius, who designed everything from teaspoons to automobile bodies, encouraged students in the direction of fresh, honest ideas. He did not want students to imitate or to become small editions of himself. But there was a difference, he pointed out, between creativity and willful independence, and cleverness in drawing, he insisted, did not necessarily mean a good design.

Besides the workshops there were courses in bookkeeping, estimating, and more or less conventional classes in architecture in which students designed buildings, made models, and analyzed old masters. In design classes, Gropius constantly related architecture to industry but admonished his students to master the machine and use it only as a means for freeing the mind.

After a training period in handiwork and design, students had to submit to an examination by masters of the Bauhaus faculty and by the Chamber of Handicrafts. If they passed this they received a Journeyman's diploma and became trade apprentices. To earn a Master's diploma they had to undergo a period of training in actual building.

Despite the burdens of administration of the Bauhaus and of teaching, Gropius carried on some building projects. These included houses in Berlin and Zehlendorf, a theater in Jena, a paper factory and a warehouse in Alfeld. On many of these projects he had collaborators—most often Adolph Meyer, who had been with him since prewar days. Meyer's death was a great loss to him.

Whenever possible, Gropius used students as assistants on his own projects. To these students he constantly pointed out that usefulness must be coupled with beauty, and creative talent with strength of character.

Although engulfed in activities, Gropius was often lonely. While he was in Hannover, Germany, to give a lecture, he met Cologne-born Ise Frank. Ise had beauty and intelligence and showed a deep, sympathetic interest in Walter and his dreams for the Bauhaus. A deep sense of companionship developed, and they were married in 1923. Ise helped him face the problems that were multiplying in connection with the school.

Gropius had assembled one of the most distinguished faculties ever housed under one roof, but the work of his staff excited abuse because it was modern. Conservatives charged that Gropius and his colleagues were Socialists. Rumors and false accusations made it difficult to get the funds needed for the state-supported school. To tide the Bauhaus over one financial crisis, Gropius sold a valuable family heirloom—linens and table service that had belonged to Napoleon.

Open houses, lectures by the staff, exhibits of student products, and a book written by Gropius and Lázló Moholy-Nagy, Hungarian designer and painter, explaining the work of the Bauhaus, won some friends, but the ridicule continued. He could endure criticism and misunderstanding, Walter told Ise, but he could not cope with continued governmental indolence as to funds and the renewed charges of socialism. To faculty and students he announced that the Bauhaus would be closed.

Students begged Gropius to reopen the school elsewhere. After newspapers headlined the rift between him and the government, offers came from four cities to make funds available for a bigger, better Bauhaus. Gropius chose Dessau, a factory town some sixty miles from Berlin. He was attracted by the beautiful natural surroundings and by the attitude of the courageous, energetic mayor who guaranteed a site and building funds.

Most of the former faculty and students moved to Dessau in the

73 □

spring of 1925 to begin building activities. On the day the new Bauhaus-Dessau was dedicated, Gropius glowed with pride. The tall dormitory, the reinforced-concrete and brick administration building with glass curtain walls, the flat-roofed shop and classroom wings gave striking contrasts, but the buildings had been unified through passages, bridges, and courts. Facilities included an auditorium, library exhibition hall, and student canteen.

There were separate duplexes for the faculty. The house Gropius had designed for Ise and himself stood in a pine woods a few hundred yards away from the main building.

The Bauhaus prospered in its new location. Gropius added a department of typography and brought in specialists in construction. Because students now lived at the school, rules had to be established. Gropius stood for complete freedom for the individual, but by freedom he did not mean Bohemianism. When students adopted weird, arty dress, he put a stop to it.

With the Bauhaus on an even keel again, Gropius entered into projects aside from administration. He studied the possibilities of prefabrication and became enthusiastic about the use of standardized parts because they could provide higher quality for lower costs.

But when the German government commissioned him to build a large housing unit in Dessau-Törten he rejected the idea of complete prefabrication with each house exactly like its neighbor.

"Component units are all very well," he told the government officials, "but homes are a personal affair and must have an individual appearance."

The Dessau-Törten settlement attracted attention not only because of the ingenious and varied use of prefabricated parts but also because Gropius made use of concrete on a mass-production scale.

At about the same time he was designing the Total Theater for his client Erwin Piscator. Both Walter and Ise had an interest in drama, and with friends who were actors had often discussed a plan for a theater that would do away with the separation between actors and audience. Gropius' Total Theater with its oval turntable stage gave the audience intimate relationship to the actors. Black Friday, which worsened Germany's already bad financial condition, killed the Total Theater, but the design became famous.

Projects such as the Total Theater never took Gropius' attention away from the Bauhaus for very long. He entered into the recreational life of the students as well as their work days. Bauhaus evenings might include a dance recital, a costume party, a concert, or a lecture by a famous architect, musician, or writer.

Informal discussions were frequent. A modest man himself, Gropius stressed the importance of humility. He had much to say about teamwork and willingness to make a contribution for the sake of the whole. Students respected him and made much of his birthday each year, presenting him with a gift album and original work done in the shops.

Around 1927, Gropius was finding it almost impossible to keep the school functioning smoothly and meet all the extra demands made on him. For the Werkbund exposition that year he designed a housing project. The fair itself, with city planning as its theme, renewed Gropius' interest in this kind of architecture.

"I'm keen to work out some of my ideas," he told Ise. "But I have so little time for designing."

The pressure increased. When the school had moved to Dessau the mayor had been liberal with funds, but shaky city finances now made support a problem. Adolf Hitler, who was rapidly gaining prestige, disliked modern architecture and called upon Germans to boycott it.

The Bauhaus did have some backers. An association known as Friends of the Bauhaus with such well-known members as the poet Franz Werfel and the scientist Albert Einstein gave both financial and moral support.

But the never-ending struggle for money, the misunderstandings, and the ill will wore Gropius down. Then posters began to appear in Dessau calling upon citizens to protest against the degenerates and Bolshevists at the Bauhaus. Some of the attacks were directed at Gropius personally. Early in 1928 he decided to turn the school over to Hannes Meyer, head of the Department of Architecture, and go back to private practice.

On the day Gropius sent his resignation to the municipal government, he delayed giving the news to the students because they were having a party that night. At the party, the students were in crazy high spirits, but at midnight a senior student suddenly halted the band. Then he walked over to Gropius. "Posters announcing your resignation are being displayed on the streets," he said. "Gropius, there is no one to fill your shoes. You ought not to leave us."

Touched by the student's loyalty, but also embarrassed, Gropius walked to the center of the hall to explain why he was resigning and to voice his regrets. After he had finished, students rushed forward and hoisted him to their shoulders. Misty-eyed, he kept telling himself that the Bauhaus would live on. But leaving the school was one of the hardest things he had ever done. He had put his heart into the Bauhaus. Within its walls he had formed deep friendships.

Newspapers and architectural magazines publicized his resignation and praised the Bauhaus as an outstanding center of architecture and design. One editor commented that its publications, exhibits, lectures, products, and graduates had had an influence out of all proportion to the size of the school.

Among Gropius' first designs after he returned to private practice in Berlin was a Municipal Employment Bureau for Dessau. Versatile and imaginative, he also designed shops, bodies for Adler cars, and stoves for the Frank Company.

Gropius also built the first slablike, multistory apartment house in Germany. When he planned houses or apartments, he was concerned with much more than a roof that would not leak; he felt obligated to create a happy climate for his clients.

His work won attention. He was elected to honorary membership in Kokusai Kenchiku Kiokai of Tokyo and to the vice presidency of the Congrès Internationale d'Architecture Moderne. Hannover Institute of Technology conferred an honorary degree. And he was a member of the Board of Experts, Reichs Research Institute for Economy in Building.

In 1930 the Salon des Artistes Décorateurs invited the German Werkbund to send a display of industrial products for an exhibition to be held in the Grand Palais in Paris. Because Gropius had previously staged a very successful outdoor exhibit in Berlin, the Werkbund asked him to take charge.

He set up the exhibit in the form of the community center of an apartment house, complete with swimming pool, dance floor, library, and play areas. It won favorable comments in the Parisian press. The German ambassador gave an elaborate reception to honor Gropius and other leading architects and artists.

Back in Berlin, however, Gropius encountered increasing coolness and hostility from the Nazis, although he still retained his post on the board of the Federal Housing Research Institute.

Shortly after Hitler took over the government, the board of the Werkbund tried to decide on their stand. The secretary-general suggested a compromise. Gropius refused to support Hitler's policies in any way and resigned from the board.

After she heard of this action, Ise said quietly, "The time has come to leave."

Gropius knew that, outspoken as he was in his views, he would never be at peace living in a Hitler-dominated Germany. But he loved the real Germany.

"Our home is here," he protested to Ise. "Our friends, and—" He could not go on. What, he asked himself, was best for Ise and for his small daughter Beate, adopted after her mother, who was Walter's sister-in-law, had died.

"We can return when Hitler is deposed," said Ise.

"You'll never be able to get passports," friends told Gropius.

"Hitler may ridicule you, but he does not let talent leave the country."

This Gropius knew to be true. But a way to escape opened up when an invitation came to read a paper at an international theater conference in Rome. He asked the sponsors to send him tickets for the family that would have Berlin-Rome-London as their destination instead of Berlin-Rome-Berlin.

"Once we're in London," he told Ise, "we can decide on our next move."

After the conference in Rome, Gropius and his family left for England. There he collaborated with E. Maxwell Fry, a modern architect who had greatly inspired his colleagues by urging them to create workable, interesting buildings to replace worn-out relics.

Gropius and Fry built several houses in London and Kent and also designed Impington College, a secondary day school and community center for Cambridgeshire.

Under less pressure than he had been for years, Gropius not only designed but wrote a book entitled *The New Architecture and the Bauhaus*. The Royal Institute of British architects, impressed by his book and his buildings, elected him to membership.

In 1937, Harvard University invited him to become Senior Professor of Architecture in the Graduate School of Design. Before he left for America, fellow architects gave him a farewell dinner presided over by the distinguished writer H.G. Wells. Herbert Read offered the toast: "Gropius belongs to the world."

Gropius felt as if he belonged to no world at all as he and his family sat in an oyster bar in Grand Central Station eating their first meal in America. Here he was, a man of fifty-four who should be at the apex of his career. Instead he was in an alien land beginning all over again.

Before he took up his duties at Harvard, Gropius spoke to the Architectural League of New York.

"I have come as a pupil as well as a teacher," he told them, in English flavored with a German accent.

He asked that he not be tagged with the Bauhaus label or with the International Style label that American architects had applied to Bauhaus products.

"My intention," he said, "is not to introduce students to a style but to a method of approach. It would be an absolute horror for me if my appointment at Harvard would result in the multiplication of a fixed idea of Gropius architecture."

At Harvard, he found familiar faces. Many Bauhaus students had followed him, and his friend Marcel Breuer had been appointed as Research Associate in the Department of Architecture. Breuer, formerly a student at the Bauhaus, now became a trusted colleague. Frank and friendly, he had views similar to those of Gropius.

Gropius respected methods and attitudes more than information, but he did not try to turn everything upside down at Harvard. From his students he demanded originality but frowned on sensational individualism in buildings and their builders. Architects he said, should plan buildings in keeping with the technical, social, and economic conditions of their society. Therefore, Romanesque buildings were out of place in a skyscraper society. The architect has an obligation, he said, to create beautiful buildings of lasting value, but he also has a moral obligation to contribute to democracy and play a role as a responsible citizen.

Gropius took a deep personal interest in his students. If he glimpsed hidden talent, he was very patient in developing it. Because he respected the viewpoint of others, students confided in him. He gave them faith in themselves and in their world. Gropius' authoritative quietness and his friendly yet decisive approach won the confidence of superiors as well as students.

In 1938 he became a member of the American Institute of Architects and chairman of the Department of Architecture of Harvard's Graduate School of Design. Some criticized the appointment, because they resented having the post go to an "alien" and a "radical artist."

How did he feel about the United States by now? asked reporters. Standards here tend to be superficial, Gropius replied, and he had been amazed to find that Americans seemed to regard the teaching of architecture as of less importance than actual designing. But he liked the United States very much and wanted to make it his permanent home.

As a site for that home, he selected the crest of an orchard-draped hill not far from Walden Pond near Lincoln, Massachusetts. Gropius had already lived in Lincoln a year and had studied the site.

Because buildings in the area were frame, Gropius designed a frame house with large porches. A long window wall that took in both living room and dining space opened out into the garden and a view of woods and hills. Through the glass, the family often saw strutting pheasant cocks and colorful songbirds. A cast-iron spiral stairway permitted thirteen-year-old Beate to get from her second-floor room into the garden. The house, when completed, attracted a steady stream of viewers.

Gropius, in partnership with Breuer, also designed other houses in the East. Between designs he liked to ride horseback or play ping-pong with Ise, but the bulk of his time was taken up by professional duties at Harvard.

During the latter part of 1938, Gropius worked hard to prepare an exhibit titled "The Bauhaus, 1919–1928," requested by the Museum of Modern Art. With the help of Herbert Bayer and Moholy-Nagy he rounded up tubular chairs, textiles, pottery, stained glass, and objects of stone, wood, paper, and clay that had been fashioned at the Bauhaus.

"Remember?" Gropius kept saying to Ise as he recalled some object he had not been allowed to bring out of Germany and which he now wished he had for the exhibit.

To tell the story of the Bauhaus, Gropius prepared a book that served as a catalogue for the exhibit. Ise, who always shared in all phases of his personal and professional life, helped with the writing. After the show closed in January, 1939, it went on a tour across the country.

The outbreak of World War II saddened Gropius. Although he had no sympathy for Hitler's goals, he knew old friends would now be subjected to deprivation and suffering. It was hard for him to concentrate on his teaching, but he gradually revamped the architecture program at Harvard. No student could graduate until he had worked six months on a construction job. Gropius was an outspoken critic of shoddy work but gave generous recognition to superior accomplishments.

Because of the growing importance of cities, he integrated courses in town planning and landscape architecture with more conventional courses. Cities, he said, should express the noblest thoughts of man instead of becoming wastelands of fakery and ugliness. His ideas had an impact not only at Harvard but also in the New Bauhaus (Institute of Design) in Chicago which he had helped his friend Moholy-Nagy to set up.

In 1941 the United States government commissioned Gropius to build a defense housing project for the employees of an aluminum factory on a hilly Pennsylvania site of New Kensington, near Pittsburgh. Gropius and his collaborator Breuer turned out two hundred and fifty row houses with brick walls at the cost of $3,280 per unit.

Honors had begun coming to Gropius. Harvard University awarded him an honorary M.A. degree. The Harvard chapter of Phi Beta Kappa made him an honorary member. He became a member of the American Society of Planners and Architects and a fellow of the American Academy of Arts and Sciences.

A collection of articles Gropius had written over a period of years for newspapers and magazines were reprinted in his book *Scope of Total Architecture*. In it he flayed the lack of independence of thought and action. People, he said, had come to rely on quantity instead of quality, on expediency instead of conviction.

"I believe," he wrote, "the creation of beauty and the forming of values and standards to be the innermost desire of a human being and that this moves him more deeply and lastingly than the satisfactions of comfort."

In another book *Rebuilding Our Communities*—the text of a lecture given in Chicago—Gropius appealed for over-all blueprints in city planning which would avoid a riot of styles, materials, colors. To emphasize his points he included over forty illustrations of good and bad town planning.

Shortly after the end of World War II, Gropius joined with seven young architects—three of them former students—to form The Architects Collaborative (T.A.C.) in which he hoped to get away from the idea of boss and employees and build a team of equal partners. He had often said in the past, "The result from a well-oiled team is greater than the sum of its ideas." But teamwork, he thought, must leave room for individual initiative and differences. This team functioned smoothly because Gropius had chosen individuals who did not belong to the "I, me, mine" cult.

Although affiliated with The Architects Collaborative, Gropius continued to carry out personal projects. He was a consultant on a renovation plan involving a seven-mile-square area on Chicago's South Side, and he helped design the Greensboro, North Carolina, plant for the Container Corporation of America.

With Konrad Wachsmann he founded the General Panel Corporation, set up to provide prefabricated houses and standardized parts that could be assembled vertically or horizontally. Gropius still insisted, however, that prefabrication should never be used for dull multiplication of standardized parts.

Although interested in prefabrication and housing developments, Gropius had to give more and more of his time to The Architects Collaborative. All the architects involved worked on an equal partner basis but assigned one person as job captain for each building project. Gropius served as captain when the group took on the job of designing the Harvard Graduate Center, a complex with seven dormitories that would house 575 students.

The two- and three-story dormitories were built of reinforced concrete and glass with buff-colored brick facing. Critics did not like the crisp style, the bare walls, but the Center earned the gold medal award of the Architectural League of New York.

Other honors came to Gropius. The CIAM (Congrès Internationale d'Architecture Moderne, of which he was still vice president) invited him to address them at meetings in Bridgewater, England, and Bergamo, Italy, and elsewhere. Western Reserve University bestowed an honorary Doctor of Science degree. He held honorary fellowships in the Society of Industrial Artists of London and the Society of Mexican Architects.

The Royal Society of Art named Gropius Honorary Royal Designer for Industry, and the Cercle D'Études Architecturales of Paris accorded him honorary membership. *Architecture d'Aujourd'hui* devoted an entire issue to Gropius' work. In 1951 he was the recipient of the Howard Myers Memorial Award of five hundred dollars given by the Architectural League of New York. The following year, the Boston Institute of Contemporary Art, in conjunction with Harvard and M.I.T., honored Gropius and the Bauhaus in an exhibition of plans for cities, models and photographs of buildings, and paintings of Bauhaus colleagues. Later, the exhibit toured the country.

That same year, Gropius, who had turned sixty-nine, decided it was time to step aside at Harvard and let a younger man take over. His resignation received wide publicity. Editors were unanimous in asserting that Gropius had made the Harvard School of Architecture one of the best in the world.

Gropius had retired from Harvard, but he had not retired from architecture. With his partners in The Architects Collaborative, he worked on schools and housing developments in the New England states, including a twenty-acre group of houses at Lexington, Massachusetts. He served as chairman of the "Panel of Five" international architects who were advisers for the building of UNESCO headquarters in Paris.

He wrote articles, several of which dealt with housing for tomorrow. Individual houses, he agreed, offered more peace, privacy, and ease in supervision of children, but they were expensive, time consuming, and made commuting distances longer. In concentrated population centers, high-rise apartments would be the solution. They could offer a maximum of air, sun, community facilities, and open park land.

In an article "The Curse of Conformity" written for the *Saturday Evening Post*, Gropius criticized the conformity imposed by mass production. It stifled independence, he said. "We are beginning to realize," he wrote, "that some important ingredients are missing in our brave new world—beauty and inner resourcefulness."

On his seventieth birthday, May 18, 1953, Chicago architects honored Gropius at a large dinner at the Blackstone Hotel in Chicago. Mies van der Rohe sketched a bit of Gropius' life and ended, "I do not have to tell you that Gropius is one of the greatest architects of our time, as well as the greatest educator in our field; you know that too. But what I want to say, and what you may not know, is that he was always a gallant fighter in the never-ending battle for new ideas."

Gropius, still clear-eyed and acting like a young man in a hurry, was deeply touched by the tributes of Mies and of other friends, students, and colleagues.

"The coming years," he said, "should be the busiest and best fulfilled of my entire life."

During those years in the 1950's, Gropius crossed and recrossed oceans and continents, usually with Ise at his side. Always as he traveled he looked for architectural developments, but he also looked for ways architects might help to unite the people of the world. He believed that sharing native gifts would do much to build a more durable world order.

In São Paulo, Brazil, Gropius received the Grand Prix International d'Architecture awarded each second year to the architect whose work has played a high important role in the development of contemporary architecture. During his travels he was often asked what a young man should do to prepare himself for a career in architecture. "Work as an assistant on a construction project," he would tell them. "Then take a full curriculum in an acknowledged school of architecture." The young architect, he believed, should become versatile in design, techniques, and economy and should give attention to city planning as well as buildings.

On a visit to Japan on a grant given by the Rockefeller Foundation, Gropius was much interested in the work of young architects—particularly that of Kenzo Tange. In honor of Gropius, Japanese architects established a Gropius Society. The Far East Society of Architecture made him an honorary member and awarded their Silver Medal of Achievement.

As he left Japan, Gropius carried with him the impression that beauty was a basic requirement of Japanese life. Westerners could do well, he thought, to adopt this goal instead of always seeking the practical, scientific, or comfortable solution.

As Gropius' buildings, his writings, his thoughts became widely known, the tempo of recognition stepped up. He received honorary degrees from North Carolina State College, the University of Sydney in Australia, the University of Brazil, and other institutions. He was made honorary member of many architectural societies from Peru to the Philippines. A seventy-fifth birthday committee organized by alumni of the Harvard Graduate School of Design had a celebration on his birthday and voted to raise funds to promote a series of annual lectures at Harvard in his honor.

In June of 1959, he went to New Orleans to accept the Gold Medal of the American Institute of Architects. He had played many roles, Gropius said in his acceptance speech—architectural revolutionary, enemy alien, university egghead. Now he was beginning to pick up a career that had begun in Germany. He appealed to fellow architects to help raise the general level of responsiveness to spiritual and esthetic values.

Awards and travel took only a fraction of Gropius' time. He served as design consultant for the Pan-American Building—a fifty-nine-story building that would be the world's largest commercial structure. With The Architects Collaborative he planned a housing project for West Berlin and the John F. Kennedy Building for Boston. Gropius, Robert S. McMillan, and H. Morse Payne, Jr., undertook a plan for the entire campus for a university of 12,000 students at Baghdad, Iraq. They envisioned a cluster of air-conditioned buildings set close together to overshadow each other. Concrete walls would cover the combined theater, auditorium, and mosque. Fountains drawing water from the nearby Tigris River would splash in garden courts.

While Gropius was working on the plan for the university, there was a change in the government of Iraq. Would the new government carry out the policies of the former? Gropius and his colleagues decided it would be best if he took designs and models of the buildings and flew to Baghdad to confer with the new premier Abdul Karim Kassem. The premier studied the designs at length.

Finally he said, "I have only one objection. I'd like to have it bigger."

Gropius smiled. "Expansion is easy," he said.

The University of Baghdad, when completed, drew much favorable comment. "A kind of poetry," said one observer.

□ 86

United States Embassy, Athens, Greece, by Walter Gropius. Photograph by Louis Reens, courtesy The Architects Collaborative.

This project and others won additional laurels. In England in 1961 Gropius was feted at a reception at Buckingham Palace. Afterward the Duke of Edinburgh presented him with the Prince Albert Gold Medal of Britain's Royal Society of Arts.

In Germany, as he traveled from city to city, Gropius recalled the days when his architecture had been derided by the Nazis and he had stood almost alone in fighting for his ideals. He was alone no longer. Previously he had received a number of awards in this country, including one presented by the President of the University of Hamburg for "furtherance of supernational thought and humanitarian efforts." The President of the Federal Republic of Germany had bestowed "The Grand Cross of Merit with Star."

Now, at a ceremony at Frankfort, Gropius received the Goethe Prize, awarded for the first time to an architect. The citation accompanying the award declared that Gropius, by means of buildings and writing, had given direction to the architecture of the industrial age and had influenced its development.

At home, Columbia University honored Gropius, Mies van der Rohe, Le Corbusier, and Frank Lloyd Wright in a "Four Great Makers" ceremony. For Gropius, the "making" of buildings went on at a hectic pace.

Before he had seen the completion of the university at Baghdad, he was going ahead with a synagogue in Baltimore and the United States Embassy in Athens, Greece.

"Make it dignified, but friendly and inviting," an official in the State Department told Gropius.

The three-story building ringed with columns was constructed around a square inner courtyard. Blue ceramic tile enclosed the ground floor. Because the site was only a mile from the famed Parthenon, Gropius had chosen the same kind of marble that had been used there to sheathe the Embassy columns. Greeks and Americans alike praised the building and referred to it as a "good neighbor for the Parthenon."

In January, 1962, Gropius went to New York to receive the Kaufmann International Design Award administered by the Institute of International Education. At the ceremonies at the St. Regis Hotel, he received a monetary award of twenty-thousand dollars and a crystal symbol by the Danish architect and designer Finn Juhl. Speakers pointed out that Gropius' principles had influenced almost every school of design in the world. He had helped countless individuals discover their potentialities.

Gropius, in his acceptance speech, challenged teachers to supply the younger generation with the independent judgment and the moral stamina needed to enable them to rise above false values. While Gropius was in New York for the award, a representative of *Newsweek* interviewed him. Questioned about quality in architecture, he said it was hard to inject quality into a commercial culture.

For Gropius' eightieth birthday in May, 1963, Mrs. Gropius, colleagues, and former students assembled at the Harkness Commons which he had designed.

"A functional birthday cake!" Ise exclaimed when a cake roughly constructed along the lines of the Bauhaus buildings was brought in.

Friends also gave him a Harvard chair, a rocking chair, and an album of letters and photographs. After the luncheon, the party went to see an exhibition of Gropius' works.

The word Bauhaus had been featured on the exhibit.

"You see," he said to Ise and others standing beside him, "the label which I did not want to be tagged with has stuck."

"You should be proud of it," said one of the group. "It is one of the great educational inventions of our time."

Gropius had taken pride in the Bauhaus, but the Bauhaus was part of the past—not part of the past in the sense of being dead, because as a method, an approach, it was still alive. But he was looking ahead and hoping for a better relationship between beauty and function.

89 □

He was also looking forward to having more time with Ise and Beate, who had married Charles Forberg, a New York architect. Their two lively daughters had added a new interest in Gropius' life. But time continued to be at a premium as new projects were presented to him.

In 1965 he was busy on a five-million-dollar plant for the world-famous Rosenthal China Company on the outskirts of Selb, Germany. To provide for future expansion Gropius designed exterior walls of prefabricated concrete panels that could be dismantled and reassembled in new combinations. Gropius welded art with craftsmanship by planning walls with a mosaic of lively colors at the ends of aisles of machinery. Employees could relax in a bright lounge with songbirds and a greenhouse to give an outdoor atmosphere.

Gropius' architecture has not possessed eruptive inventiveness, but he has earned the right to be called one of the few great pioneers of modern architecture. His buildings in the United States, Germany, Greece, Iraq, and England will endure. His principles will be practiced by the students he taught so effectively—students like Paul Rudolph and I. Ming Pei, who became leaders in their profession.

His standards of design will continue to influence fabrics, furniture, and city planning from the islands of Japan to the steaming valley of the Tigris.

Builder of buildings, Gropius was also a builder of values. The "good of society" always has run through his conversation. "The foremost need of the ideal architect," he has said, "is high human qualities." Walter Gropius had these qualities. Le Corbusier said of him, "To speak of Walter Gropius is to speak of a friendship founded upon dignity, loyalty, generosity, upon his warm heart, his intelligence and talent."

And José Luis Sert, Dean of the Harvard Graduate School, has referred to him as "A great human being as well as a great artist."

FOUR

MIES VAN DER ROHE

Less Is More

At an early age, Ludwig Mies van der Rohe had a job as runner on a construction project. One of his duties was to go and get boiling water for carpenters who wanted to make coffee. If he didn't move fast enough to please them, workmen would throw an ax or some other tool at him. But neither impatient carpenters nor the noise, dirt, and muscle strain could spoil the excitement of seeing a building take shape. Mies felt this even more keenly when he worked alongside his father, a master stone mason and proprietor of a small stone-cutting shop in Aachen, Germany. His father taught him how to lay stone upon stone with artistry and made him aware of the drawbacks and possibilities of masonry construction.

Mies could not remember a time when he had not been fascinated by buildings. Between childish games he had often paused to stare at some building that captured his attention. Each morning when he went with his mother to the old Chapel of Charlemagne, he amused himself counting stones and tracing joints.

After he finished elementary school, Mies went to a trade school for two years. But from the time he was fifteen, he worked full time as an apprentice and later as a draftsman for local designers and architects. One of his first projects was to draw ornaments later to be rendered into stucco. Because his employer did not provide drawing boards, Mies had to stand up and design on huge sheets of paper pinned to the wall.

In 1905, Mies, then nineteen, went to Berlin. The only job he could find called for designing in wood. Stone he knew; wood he did not. If he had to learn a new technique, he thought he might as well go to an expert teacher. He applied for a job at the studio of Bruno Paul, leading decorator and furniture designer. Paul took him as an apprentice.

During leisure hours, Mies read a great deal—philosophy, natural science, sociology. He was much impressed by the writings of St. Augustine and St. Thomas Aquinas and accepted many of their ideas about order and rightness.

At the age of twenty-one, ready to strike out on his own, Mies designed his first house. His temperament favored precision and thoroughness, and these qualities showed up in the carefully executed house.

Far from satisfied, he apprenticed himself to Peter Behrens. This noted designer quickened his appreciation for fine detail and taught him to place structures on wide platforms or pedestals to lend nobility. The buildings of Behrens and the distinguished architect, Karl Friedrich Schinkel, gave Mies new ideas on proportion, simplicity, and the use of glass and steel.

Mies progressed so steadily that Behrens entrusted him with supervision of construction of a series of buildings. Most important of these was the German Embassy in St. Petersburg, Russia. Later, in 1912, Behrens asked Mies to go to The Hague in Holland to dis-

Mies van der Rohe

cuss a project with his client Mme. Kröller. She had earlier commissioned Behrens to design a home that would provide a sumptuous setting for her collection of paintings. Now she wanted a model made of the house. After Mies talked with Mme. Kröller, she was so impressed with his ability that she asked him to submit his own design.

Mies never got to carry out his plans for the Kröller house because his client changed her mind about building it. But he felt his time had not been wasted. While in The Hague he had studied the buildings of the Dutch architect Hendrik Petrus Berlage. He resolved that his own buildings would have the same simplicity and integrity in the use of materials.

When Mies returned to Berlin he opened his own office. Commissions for several villas came in, but the outbreak of war interrupted his work. Because he was not a university graduate, he could not serve as an officer in the German army. During most of the conflict, he was stationed with an engineer corps in the Balkans.

In Berlin again at the end of the war, Mies found citizens in

93 □

revolt against the old form of government by kings. Architects were in revolt against styles borrowed from the past. Mies staged his own revolution. For a competition, he designed a twenty-story office building with three towers rising like a sheer cliff of crystal. The charcoal study of the skyscraper was a work of art in itself.

No architect had ever conceived a building so radically all glass, and when the design was exhibited some called it shocking. But others saw remarkable possibilities in his skin-and-bones kind of architecture in which there was a steel skeleton on the inside and a skin of glass on the outside.

Still intrigued by skyscraper construction, Mies designed a second one that had a glass façade intended to reflect itself. He also drew a study for a concrete and glass building in which floor supports were provided by slabs cantilevered outward. Other features were ribbon windows—an uninterrupted horizontal bank of windows—and an entrance without ornamentation. One observer said that behind the simplicity of the building there was a host of carefully developed details as unobtrusive as the stitching on a well-tailored suit.

The drawings of skyscrapers and of houses—one a country villa —were exhibited widely and pushed Mies to the forefront of the modern movement, but they did not win him clients. Uncertainties in the political situation and wild inflationary cycles handicapped all architects in Germany. Mies had an additional problem—the public for the most part regarded him as a visionary rather than a practical architect.

At first, his confidence was unshaken. After all, he had grown up putting stone on stone and felt sure he knew the problems involved in building. But as the years passed with no really important assignment, Mies almost began to doubt himself. Shortly after his thirty-eighth birthday, when a friend complimented him on his building, he replied with a wry smile, "I have built nothing except a reputation."

That reputation finally won friends. Commissions began to come in. These were mostly for private dwellings, but Mies also designed a low-cost housing project for the city of Berlin.

All of his houses looked as if they belonged to their setting and reflected unusual care in the selection of materials. To get evenness at corners, he calculated all dimensions in brick lengths and occasionally went so far as to separate overfired from underfired bricks, using the long in one dimension and the short in another. Sometimes he went to kilns to choose his own bricks. He never covered them with stucco because to him this seemed dishonest. The homes and housing projects built in Berlin and in other German cities proved that Mies did indeed know how to design buildings that would stand the test of time.

During the same period, Mies wrote a number of articles and headed the architectural section of the Novembergruppe, an organization for the promotion of modern art. To give architects a rallying point exclusively their own, he founded the Zehner Ring, which had as its purpose the offsetting of official prejudice against the modern movement.

In the late 1920's, Mies gave much of his energy to the Deutscher Werkbund, which had been formed two decades earlier to promote high standards of craftsmanship and industrial design. When the group began planning for the erection of several houses for the 1927 exposition at Stuttgart, Mies was asked to take charge and coordinate the contributions of Europe's leading architects.

During construction of the Werkbund housing, he lived at the site. Besides supervising the general layout of the buildings and handling administrative duties, Mies planned a display for the glass industry and designed an apartment house with long banks of glass, prefabricated movable partitions, and a roof garden.

At the exposition, visitors received a booklet in which architects explained their entries. Some architects took pages. Mies limited his description to twelve terse lines. American architect Philip Johnson

95 □

used the label International Style to apply to the products of Mies and those other architects who relied on modern techniques and on geometric purity of form with no ornament. Johnson used this term because architecture adapted to the world of machines must also be international.

The exhibition advanced the cause of the International Style; it also advanced the cause of Mies. He had shown superb organizational skill, and his apartment building was praised as a beautiful, clean-cut achievement. Mies' contributions at the Stuttgart exhibition were noticed by governmental officials. They invited him to design the German Pavilion for the 1929 exposition in Barcelona, Spain.

"For what purpose?" Mies asked.

"France and England are putting up pavilions," he was told. "Just build one without too much glass."

In Barcelona, Mies placed a one-story pavilion upon a wide pedestal of travertine, part of which had a pool lined in black glass. Steel columns sheathed in chrome supported the hovering roof. At one end the green marble walls that enclosed the interior seemed to slide out, under, and beyond the roof plane to form an enclosed sculpture court the floor of which was largely taken up by another reflecting pool. On a small base in this pool, Mies placed a statue by Georg Kolbe.

For the interior, Mies collaborated with the brilliant furniture designer Lilly Reich. They used free-standing walls of travertine, marble, onyx, and glass to set off exquisitely made pieces of furniture. Mies had already designed and exhibited steel chairs. Now he used one made of steel bands in single and reverse curves. Everything about it—thickness of metal, radius of curves, and size of upholstery buttons—had been calculated to the last millimeter.

Elegant materials, expert craftsmanship, the sure hand of genius made the Barcolona Pavilion a striking building and brought worldwide fame. Architectural magazines acclaimed its "brilliant execu-

German Pavilion, International Exposition, Barcelona, Spain, by Mies van der Rohe. 1929. Photograph courtesy The Museum of Modern Art.

tion, poetic vision, and architectural sculpture." Some called it the most beautiful building of our generation. Asked how he conceived of such beauty, Mies said simply that logic leads to truth and truth to beauty. After the exhibition, the Pavilion was dismantled and shipped back to Germany, but Mies was never able to find out what became of the pieces.

By then he was concentrating on plans for a house for the newly married Tugendhats in Brno, Czechoslovakia. Most dwellings at this time were austerely functional. Mies wanted to use rich materials and impart elegance. Because the site was a hilly one he treated the top of the house as the entrance floor. A glass-enclosed stairway led to the living space below, where a wall of tawny gold and white onyx defined the living room and a semicircle of ebony demarcated the dining area. Panels that could be automatically lowered into the basement converted the living room into a semi-enclosed terrace.

Mies designed all the furnishings, even to the door handles. Every single piece of furniture was placed with studied exactness to achieve maximum effect. Curtains were of black and beige raw silk and white velvet. The Tugendhat House earned plaudits as one of the finest houses ever built anywhere in the world.

In 1930 Hannes Meyer, who had succeeded Gropius as head of the Bauhaus, resigned. State officials asked Mies to accept the post as director, and he went forward, following much the same procedures as those of the founder Gropius. Mies believed that architects must understand the motives and forces of their time and create new forms, but they should not be faddists. And they should build, he said, not only on the material but the spiritual.

Mies had much to say about materials and their use. But to a student who had the idea that anyone could make a beautiful building if only he had fine wood or stone, Mies said, "What is important is not *what* but *how*." He went on to say that materials could only be given meaning and value by the architect himself.

Achievements such as an elegant white-walled house and bachelor apartment designed for the Berlin Building exhibition in 1931 led to an invitation to membership in the Prussian Academy of Arts and Sciences. Speeches, similar to the one Mies gave at a Werkbund meeting in Vienna, and exhibits of his drawings in museums around the world made his name favorably known.

But the Nazis, who had gained control of the local government in Dessau, launched malicious attacks against him. They charged that he taught un-German ideas. The solution seemed to be to move the school.

Regretfully, Mies abandoned the fine Bauhaus buildings in Dessau and set up quarters in an empty factory in Berlin. The Berlin Bauhaus had been in operation only a short time when Hitler took over as dictator of Germany. Nazi harassment redoubled. Because Mies was a man of deep-seated principles, he would not pretend to subscribe to Nazi goals just to get support for the school.

After a talk with Nazi "cultural expert" Alfred Rosenberg one evening in 1933, Mies was convinced that the school was doomed.

"The school cannot continue to exist in this atmosphere," he told his colleagues. "We are going to close it.

When his friends looked at him in consternation, Mies tried to comfort them and himself by pointing out that the Bauhaus influence would continue. The ideals and methods on which it had been founded would live and grow through the work of its students and staff, who would exhibit products, write books, and carry its methods elsewhere. But at the moment he could think only of the pain of severing ties that meant so much to him.

Although Mies closed the Bauhaus, he still made his home in Germany. At forty-seven, he thought, it would not be easy to start over again in another country. For a time he busied himself designing what he called court houses. These houses, with exterior walls of glass, were shaped in L's, T's, or I's but all of them had courts. Although these houses won acclaim, clients stopped coming. They were going to builders who followed the Nazi line.

In 1937, Mies was invited to head the School of Architecture at Chicago's Armour Institute. Frank Lloyd Wright introduced him to the trustees and faculty at a dinner in the ballroom of Palmer House in Chicago. "Ladies and gentlemen," he said, putting an arm across Mies' shoulder, "I give you Mies van der Rohe. . . . I admire him as an architect and respect him as a man."

Mies responded in German. Later, in his inaugural address as director, he said that students must have knowledge and skills. But they must also have values that would help them make the right use of facts and skills.

When he turned to setting up a course of study for Armour, Mies had help from several of his former associates at the Bauhaus who had accompanied him to this country. Among them was Ludwig Hilberseimer, architect and city planner. Mies required that students work first with wood, then with stone, then with brick, and finally with concrete and steel. Each material, he pointed out, had special characteristics that should be understood. He encouraged students to keep their designs free from fussy details, "Less is more," he kept saying.

Mies believed he could teach students how to work. He could teach techniques: give students a sense of order, principles, proportion. But what aspiring architects did with these was their problem. Only the serious and single-minded could attain the standards he set.

Two years after Mies came to Armour, the Institute merged with Lewis Institute to form the Illinois Institute of Technology, but he continued as director of the School of Architecture. President Heald, a friend and admirer, entrusted him with designing buildings for the campus that would cover eight city blocks. Construction would be carried out over a period of years.

Mies envisioned rectangular cubes of brick, steel, and glass. Although the buildings appeared simple on paper, it would take unceasing thought and work to achieve the subtle proportions and perfection he demanded of himself.

Asked if the campus buildings would look alike because they were built on the same basic plan, he replied, "There are some ten thousand species of seashells. They have the same principle, but they don't look alike."

World War II slowed the I.I.T. program and brought damage or destruction to buildings Mies had designed in Europe. A student who had been in Czechoslovakia brought him photographs of the Tugendhat House that the Nazis were using as a gymnasium. Mies, although he still had friends in Germany and many pleasant memories of life there, broke completely with his homeland and became a citizen of the United States.

After the war ended he served as President of the Congrès Internationale d'Architecture Moderne, moved ahead with I.I.T. buildings, and designed a drive-in restaurant for Indianapolis. When the Museum of Modern Art in New York asked for a retrospective exhibit of his work, Mies, with help from Philip Johnson, compiled a sizable monograph to accompany the exhibit. Although the show shocked traditionalists, it made architectural history. The September 1947 issue of *Architectural Record* said that architecture had received no higher expression in our time than the work of Mies.

Meanwhile he had met Herbert Greenwald, a real-estate investor and builder. Mies liked his idealistic philosophy and his insistence on the finest possible architecture. Together they planned the Promontory Apartments in an area of Chicago near Lake Michigan.

Mies designed a concrete-and-brick structure with impressive expanses of glass. On the principal façades he stepped back his columns at various levels and made them progressively smaller as they rose to the roof line. The result was an artistic, subtle elongation.

101 □

This building was so successful that Mies and Greenwald teamed up to build two tall apartment houses side by side at 860 Lake Shore Drive. The twin towers based on steel piers around an enclosed lobby gave the effect of standing on stilts. Vertical beams of black steel spaced about five feet apart and running the full height of the building were welded to the exterior between floor-to-ceiling windows.

The two buildings, at right angles to each other but at oblique angles to the main thoroughfare, were connected by a black steel canopy. To some the gaunt towers appeared stark, cold, ominous. But those who walked toward the towers head-on saw façades like huge mirrors that reflected sky and clouds and had beauty comparable to that of a painting.

Mies' admirers called the towers his strongest work. One said the crystal shafts were like flights of fancy. Photographs of the interiors appeared in *Life* magazine, and the twin towers became known around the world as Mies 860.

When he designed a house, Mies always had the interests of his client in mind. But he could be stubborn in insistence on what he considered best.

"I don't compromise," he said. "I would rather sell potatoes."

For Dr. Edith B. Farnsworth, a Chicago physician and Assistant Professor of Medicine at Northwestern University, he built a home on a wooden site on the Fox River near Plano, Illinois. To prevent damage from spring floods, Mies placed the house on stilts. It appeared almost to float in the air. Entrance porches were graceful and elegant, and glass walls permitted observation of sky and woodland.

No matter what other projects he might be involved in, Mies was always at work on some aspect of the I.I.T. building program. Novelty did not interest him, but he experimented constantly and revised until each tiny detail had been worked out with artistry. When someone chided him for the starkness of the I.I.T. buildings,

Crown Hall, I.I.T., Chicago, Illinois, by Mies van der Rohe. 1955. Photograph courtesy The Museum of Modern Art.

he answered, "There are good roses, but all plants cannot be roses; there are also good vegetables."

Each of the I.I.T. buildings had distinctive features. In the hallway of the Alumni Memorial Hall, there was a remarkable cantilevered stairway. The Architecture and Design Building called Crown Hall was elevated on a handsome platform with steps leading to it.

For the entire campus Mies respected the "form follows function" philosophy up to a point. But he was also aware that buildings often outlived their original function. Who could predict, he asked, what functions classrooms or laboratories built in 1955 would have in the year 2000? The only kind of building that would make sense was a flexible one in which beauty was the only permanent ingredient. Critics said Mies' I.I.T. buildings might be flexible but had little beauty. These persons had overlooked the delicate precision in detail and the dignity of the buildings.

Besides his teaching and designing duties at I.I.T., Mies was at work on a series of projects with Herb Greenwald. They added two more buildings to the 860 complex. Other glass towers rose in cities from Chicago to Brooklyn.

In 1958, after twenty years at I.I.T., Mies decided the time had come to give up his teaching. During the years he had set up an impressive architectural school and had seen dozens of former students promoted to responsible positions.

But exit from the classroom did not mean retirement from architecture. Mies was already busy on a challenging commission in New York—a thirty-eight-story building for the company of Joseph E. Seagram and Sons. The site was a block-long frontage on Park Avenue diagonally across from the green-glass and aluminum Lever House design by Gordon Bunshaft.

The Seagram company had allocated thirty million dollars for the construction. As collaborator, Mies chose his friend Philip Johnson, who had left the Museum of Modern Art to devote his full time to architectural practice.

For the Seagram Building, Mies wanted some materials that were nonexistent. He urged a glass manufacture to turn out subtly tinted topaz glass that would cut down the glare of the sun. To help him achieve a lighter, more waterproof cover for skeletal steel, the aluminum industry fabricated unusually long beams of aluminum strong enough to hold and brace large areas of glass. The partners worked with painstaking care. No doorknob, faucet, or mail chute was neglected.

The building opened in 1958. Those who came saw a tower that soared upward in an uninterrupted five-hundred-twenty-foot façade of glass. Verticality was stressed by bronze fins separating floor-to-ceiling windows. These fins gave the building the color of an old cannon.

The building was set back a hundred feet from the sidewalk to leave space for a plaza with trees, beds of greenery, fountains, and step-rimmed pools. The same care that had gone into the building was evident in the plaza with siding of green marble, tall bronze flagpole, and fountain, a model of which had been tested in a laboratory at the Massachusetts Institute of Technology.

Mrs. Phyllis Lambert, daughter of Samuel Bronfman, president of Seagram and Sons, has said of the building, "You feel its force and restfulness. Love has gone into it—love for every detail."

Architect Gordon Bunshaft commented, "That old Dutcher expresses steel and America better than anyone."

Mies credited associates with contributing much to the total success of the Seagram Building. "We helped," said Philip Johnson, "but the spirit that made it whole was that of Mies."

Mies believed that when new problems came along, he would know how to meet them. This he did with tremendous verve and patience.

While designing a building for the Cuban Compañia Ron

Bacardi, he made more than a hundred studies of the columns that would support the roof before he arrived at a plan for tapered columns that suited him. In 1959, while he was in Santiago discussing plans with Bacardi officials, his friend Herb Greenwald was killed in an airplane crash in New York. Ever since they had collaborated on the apartment buildings in Chicago, the two men had shared projects. Now the partnership of skills and ideals had been shattered. The thought of going on alone staggered Mies.

But he went ahead with plans he and Greenwald had made together, as well as with solo projects. Among these were a second structure for the Bacardi Company in Mexico City and the new Cullinan wing for the Houston Museum of Fine Arts. At the opening in February, 1959, donor Nina Cullinan said happily that Mies had made the museum look like a great stage.

Critics continued to apply the adjectives, "cold, icy, inhuman" to Mies' work, but the world which had been slow to honor him had now awakened to his gifts. Museums in many lands exhibited his designs. In Germany, where the Nazis had rejected him, the Technische Hochschule of Karlsruhe awarded him an honorary doctorate. He was selected to the Order of Merit—highest honor that includes only thirty-nine members chosen from all over the world.

Mies had previously been made an honorary corresponding member of the Royal Institute of British Architects. In the summer of 1959, he went to London to receive the Royal Gold Medal for Architecture from Queen Elizabeth II. The following year he was awarded the Gold Medal of the A.I.A. at a meeting in San Francisco. In his acceptance speech, he said he was grateful for the honor and for the opportunity to teach and work in the United States. He was, he said, often asked the question, where do we go from here? "We are," he said, "at the beginning of a new epoch, guided by a new spirit, using new tools, materials. The future is open for creative thought and action, but we must be guided by truth."

After a trip such as the one to San Francisco, Mies would

107 □

Seagram Building, New York City, by Mies van der Rohe. 1958. Photograph courtesy Seagram and Sons.

again take up his professional duties in Chicago. Afternoons he went to his austere, white-walled office where he examined drawings, scale models, and mock-ups prepared in a workshop as well equipped as a cabinet maker's. With a minimum of words to his assistants, he would indicate the changes to be made.

"Beinahe nichts—almost nothing," he would say, half to himself, as he strove toward simplicity and the best possible use of structural material. Projects were often diverse in their functions— a redevelopment housing project in Detroit, a high-rise housing development in Newark, an office building in Baltimore, a Home Federal Savings and Loan Association Building in Des Moines. If asked which of the buildings in the past was most important, Mies was likely to say, "No single building stands out. My whole life has been a search for good architecture and a search for an answer to the question, What is truth?"

In 1963, Mies had under construction a Federal Center for Chicago and a classroom building for Drake University. He was designing luxury apartments for Baltimore, a science center for Duquesne University, a museum for West Berlin, a headquarters for the German Krupp firm, and a Social Service Administration Building for the University of Chicago.

By then, Mies was being called the most elegant perfectionist of contemporary architecture. Honest in his use of materials, precise in details, a master of proportion, he had planned a major campus and changed the New York skyline. On a hill above Barcelona, he had built one of the most beautiful structures of an era. His "less is more" was heard in architectural classrooms around the world, and architects imitated his functional framework.

These achievements were honored in December, 1963, when Mies received the presidential Medal of Freedom—highest governmental recognition that can be given a civilian.

The award was as much a tribute to the man as to his buildings. Throughout his life, Mies' goal had been to create buildings that would serve humanity, not to gain a name for himself. During an interview for the *Saturday Review* in 1965, Mies was asked, "What were the most important influences on your work?"

"I thought a lot," Mies replied, "and I controlled my thoughts in my work—and I controlled my work through my thoughts. I read voraciously . . . . I worked under a few good architects."

Whatever the influences, Mies van der Rohe imbued architecture with the spiritual quality of great design because he was himself spiritual. Order, truth, self-discipline were the watchwords of his life. Because of these qualities, the name of Mies van der Rohe may well be remembered after others have been forgotten.

FIVE

ERIC MENDELSOHN

Architect in Four Countries

Eric Mendelsohn spent a miserable year as a freshman at the University of Munich. He had enrolled in economics only out of respect for his father David Mendelsohn, a self-made Russian-Polish businessman. Courses in economics convinced Eric that he would never be happy in the world of business. From the time he was five years old, he had wanted to become an architect. He could still remember the clay models he had made of the old medieval castles that dominated his home town—Allenstein, East Prussia. Now he made up his mind to tell his parents that economics seemed cold and dull to him.

The Mendelsohns were a close-knit family, and when Eric confided in them, they agreed that he should shift to architecture. Eric was enthusiastic about his courses in design. Outside the classroom his ardent, romantic nature found an outlet in dramatics. He also took part in agitation for Zionism—a movement to unite Jews from all over the world in a national homeland in Palestine. Young Zionists met in cafés for long, intense discussions on politics, culture, and the books they were reading.

Another interest, music, led to an introduction to Louise Maas, who, although still in her teens, was a fine cellist. Eric told her how his mother, a milliner before her marriage but also a gifted musician, had inspired her children to love music. He and his five brothers and sisters had all played the piano.

As graduation drew near, Eric realized that it would probably be best to get some practical experience with a mature architect. But he wanted his own office and opened one in Munich in 1911, only days after he won his Master of Arts degree.

Three years later, war broke out in Europe. Mendelsohn enlisted and served in the German army Corps of Engineers. At first, while standing guard duty at the front, he was terrified by the din of rapid fire that brought death to men all around him. But as the weeks passed, he gained confidence that the promise that stirred within him could be fulfilled and that he would survive.

Once more he began to visualize buildings and to sketch them. Paper was scarce at the front, and to economize, Mendelsohn drew tiny plans often no larger than a square inch. These had endless variety and were of a type no one had ever built. And always he saved some of his precious paper for letters to Louise. She responded with sympathy when he wrote of his longing to get back to construction instead of destruction. Eric appreciated her understanding and charm even more than her musicianship.

During the war, Mendelsohn married Louise, and when the war was over, he opened an office in Berlin. While he waited for clients to begin coming, he sketched. These drawings had so much daring, originality, and artistry that Paul Cassirer of the Cassirer's Galleries in Berlin held an exhibit. This included sketches made at the front, redrawn in poster form and titled "Architecture in Steel and Concrete."

Before the exhibit opened, Louise went to see the designs but came home looking dejected. Eric finally wrung from her the admission that Cassirer had said, "Tell your husband to take another road. He will never be able to realize such fantastic structures."

"What did you say to that?" asked Mendelsohn.

Louise was by nature a quiet person, but now her eyes flashed. "I said, 'He will!' " she replied hotly.

Louise had a wide knowledge and appreciation of the arts. If she believed in him, nothing else mattered, thought Eric. But the public sided with Cassirer. "This is fine painting, but it is not architecture," one critic said of the exhibit.

Mendelsohn still had confidence that he could build what he had drawn if he ever got the chance, but he was already thirty-one. Sometimes it took Louise's fierce devotion to keep him going.

He was encouraged when Dutch architect H. T. Wijdevald, editor of the architectural magazine *Wendingen*, asked him to lecture in Holland and also published some of his sketches. Another opportunity to prove his worth came when Mendelsohn was invited to design an Astrophysical Institute Tower at Potsdam that would provide observatory and laboratory facilities for proof of some of Albert Einstein's theories. Mendelsohn had long been an admirer of the brilliant scientist and had a deep desire to construct a building that Einstein would approve.

The Einstein Tower, with a superstructure of brick, had sweeping curves. Deep window recesses allowed an impressive play of light and shadow that symbolized something of the mystery of the universe that astronomers and physicists hoped to penetrate.

On the day Einstein and the building committee came to inspect the Tower, Mendelsohn could not tell whether the gentle, sad-eyed scientist was pleased or not. But at the end of the tour Einstein came over to Mendelsohn and whispered, "Organic!"

Nothing could have pleased him more. To Mendelsohn, organic

Eric Mendelsohn

meant unity, with one form growing out of another and with nothing appearing to be stuck on.

The Einstein Tower was an immediate success. A photograph of it got cover notice on the picture magazine, the *Berline Illustriete.*

Mendelsohn sketched with renewed confidence, but then an eye difficulty developed. Even his worst fears did not match the verdict.

"Cancer," a specialist told him. "The eye will have to be removed."

Mendelsohn was just becoming reconciled to a glass eye, which looked almost like his own, when another blow fell. The remaining eye, the surgeon told him, was weak. If he continued designing, he would almost certainly overtax his vision and lose it. For Mendelsohn the choice between loss of sight or loss of his profession was an agonizing one.

After he made up his mind to go ahead and ignore the handicap as much as possible, his exuberant optimism returned. In rapid

The Einstein Tower, Potsdam, Germany, by Eric Mendelsohn, 1921. Photograph courtesy The Bettmann Archive.

succession Mendelsohn designed an addition to the *Berliner Tageblatt* Building, a home in Berlin, residences at Charlottenburg, a hat factory in Luckenwalde, and a silk store and a power station in Silesia. He wished now that he had worked in an architectural office to gain practical experience in technical matters. But he learned on the job and his buildings were good.

To handle all the assignments coming his way, Mendelsohn kept adding assistants. One of these was a promising young Austrian, Richard Neutra. The two men worked so well together that they were soon collaborating. A design they submitted in a competition for a business center in Haifa, Palestine, won first prize.

Mendelsohn used his share of the prize money to study synagogues and skyscrapers in the United States. The experimentation he saw going on exhilarated him. He met famous architects, including Frank Lloyd Wright, took copious notes, and photographed important buildings.

Back in Germany, Mendelsohn compiled a book with seventy-seven photographs and highly individual notes which he titled *America—Architect's Picture-book*. Demands for designs limited time for further writing. To inspect progress of a textile factory he had under construction in Leningrad, Mendelsohn went to Russia. The poor quality of the work being done there shocked him.

"The builders," he wrote Louise, "ought to be rolled as thin as a piece of tin foil as a penalty for their nonrecognition of the fact that every body must exist in three dimensions."

Shortly after Mendelsohn came home, he wrote *Russia, Europe, America—An Architectural Cross-section.*

During the next few years he designed the Metalworkers' Union Administrative Building and a complex of buildings for the Woga Company in Berlin—shops, a six-story bachelor hotel, a block of flats, and a theater.

The Nazis publicly criticized Mendelsohn because he was a so-called radical architect and because he was a Jew. But commissions still poured in, and he had to add more draftsmen and assistants. At one time he had as many as forty employees. After Richard Neutra moved to the United States, Mendelsohn relied more and more on the Austrian architect Johannes Schreiner, who was ingenious in the solution of structural problems.

Designs for department stores often occupied the staff. Up to then, European department stores had often been clumsy imitations of native Renaissance palaces with oversized windows for display. Mendelsohn's stores featured cantilevered glass surfaces and horizontal bands of windows. The use of curved glass stairhalls gave grace to some of the buildings. The simple but handsome Salman Schocken

Schocken Department Store, Stuttgart, Germany, by Eric Mendelsohn. 1926. Photograph courtesy The Musuem of Modern Art.

store at Chemnitz had a curved front. Some predicted that because of Mendelsohn's tender attention to luxurious details, the store would rank high among architectural masterpieces of the twentieth century. He also built stores located at Nuremburg, Stuttgart, Berlin, Breslau, and Duisburg.

Besides department stores, Mendelsohn designed the "Three Patriarchs' Lodge" at Tilsit, East Prussia, a cemetery at Königsberg, and a Youth Center at Essen. Plans drawn for Lindenstreet. and Alexanderplatz gave evidence of his interest in city planning. A design for the Cathedral Square at Magdeburg won first prize.

Busy as he was with public buildings, Mendelsohn took time to plan a home for his wife and daughter Esther on a narrow lot in a quiet suburban street where Grünwald Forest joins Havel Lake. The long house of brick and steel was built in three levels with glass walls that gave an impressive view of the lake and a slope covered with birch, oak, fir, and flowers. At the push of a button, glass partitions sank into the basement that housed servant's quarters, storerooms, and machinery.

Although Louise put marriage ahead of her music, she still played cello with artistry, and Eric made the music room the largest one in the house. In this room and elsewhere, beautifully designed cabinets covered everything from music to telephones.

Mendelsohn liked to share his home with his family and friends, but he spent most of his time in his workroom on the top floor. He designed with such zeal that he rarely took time off for lunch and frequently ate dinner while seated in front of a drafting board. Because music gave him a sense of release, he often sketched to the accompaniment of records.

His preliminary drawings included everything that would follow—interior as well as exterior. He then combined these into three-dimensional designs and laboriously perfected models.

During the early 1930's, Mendelsohn built houses, a power station, and a zinc factory in Germany and stores in Ostroava, Czechoslovakia, and Oslo, Norway. Most outstanding of his buildings during this period was Columbus House, an office building in Berlin with a sheltered garden restaurant on the roof. Glazed bands emphasized the horizontal lines. Architectural publications praised the "singing lines and graceful circles" of Mendelsohn's buildings. Some went so far as to call him the first really successful modern architect.

Publicity, prizes, buildings, and books—*The Creative Spirit of the World Crisis* and *New House, New World*—brought Mendelsohn to the height of his fame. The Prussian Academy of Arts in Berlin elected him to membership. Lectures in Greece, England, Spain, Switzerland, and France won admirers.

But at home, the Nazis who condemned him were growing in numbers and influence. The freedom and individuality which Mendelsohn valued were being stamped out. Persons of Jewish extraction were increasingly subjected to barbarities.

One day Mendelsohn could not keep his mind on his work. He went to the front of his house and looked down at the flowers and the delicate leaves of the birch trees. Customarily the sweet scent of growing things, the sight of water instilled peace, but today he felt only turmoil. The Nazis, he thought, were forging a new kind of country. How could his art, his beliefs, ever survive in Hitler's Germany?

Mendelsohn was so tired from strains connected with his work that the idea of starting over in another land overwhelmed him. Furthermore, all the traditions of his life were German and he had fought to defend these traditions. But to stay on now would be to choose death. Heavy of heart, he returned to his drafting board.

A short time later, Louise and Eric decided to leave the country and to live temporarily in Holland. On the day in 1933 that Mendelsohn, his wife, and daughter left Germany, Hitler seized control of the government. Although Mendelsohn deplored what had happened to his homeland, he had a deep faith in the goodness of man and did not let his own experiences make him bitter. He could even summon a wry kind of humor when he learned that his Metalworkers Union Building had become the headquarters for the Nazi Labor Front and that the Gestapo had moved into Columbus House.

Tired of designing, Mendelsohn turned to writing and public speaking. When he went on a lecture tour in England, Sir Charles Reilly referred to him as the most brilliant architect in Europe. The enthusiasm of fellow architects, including his refugee friend Walter Gropius, rekindled Mendelsohn's own ardor.

"I thought I was tired of architecture," he told Louise. "Instead I was just tired."

Everywhere Mendelsohn traveled in England, new-found friends urged him to stay. The Home Office extended his original permit from five weeks to five years. The Mendelsohns then decided to move to London. Eric opened an office with a younger architect, Serge Chermayeff, whom he had met several years before. The partners collaborated on several residences.

One of these was a large, luxurious house alongside one built by Gropius and Fry and connected by a common garden. Mendelsohn and Chermayeff also won the competition for a design for a municipal summer resort and recreation center at Bexhill on the Suxsex coast. The low, horizontal, glass-and-steel building called the De La Warr Pavilion harmonized with the sea beyond it. At the south there was a spiral staircase enveloped in a glass shell.

The Duke of York came for the opening of the facilities, which when complete included a ballroom, library, concert hall, restaurant, terrace, and swimming pool. Architects and the public ranked the Pavilion as one of the finest modern buildings in England.

When the eminent Zionist statesman and scientist Chaim Weizmann invited Mendelsohn to redesign his residence at Rehoboth, near Tel Aviv, Mendelsohn made a trip to Palestine. Before he sketched a plan for any building, he always studied the site, but he did unusually careful research for this house because of his personal interest in Zionism and in Weizmann, whom he had known for some time.

After thorough study of the climate and the countryside, with its domed hills, parasol pines, and olive and orange trees, Mendelsohn designed a stately house with a circular staircase tower in the center. A covered patio flanked by the library and drawing room faced a swimming pool. The rest of the house extended into a half-wild garden and sanctuary for birds.

The Weizmann House led to other commissions in Palestine. Public buildings here presented many new problems. Authorities expected architects to make new structures blend with the old ones, mostly Byzantine or Moslem in style. Stone was the approved building material.

Although Mendelsohn used up-to-date techniques, he made his buildings native in spirit. In Europe he had tried to expose clients to the sun. Now he learned to use devices such as deep-set windows that would protect them from excessive glare.

The Medical Center built for Hadassah University on Mount Scopus outside Jerusalem had cream-colored limestone walls. The three parts—medical school, school of nursing, and hospital—were connected through the use of terraces, curved walls, gardens, and pergolas. A glass wall enclosed a large, handsome entrance hall protected by projecting wings and a veranda with a metal grille roof. Mendelsohn also designed the British Government Hospital at Haifa.

Because Palestinian projects demanded so much of his time, he dissolved his partnership with Chermayeff, but he still considered England his home. He so admired the liberty-loving English people that he took out citizenship papers.

Whenever Mendelsohn was in his adopted country, he preferred to spend his time with his wife and daughter, but he did make a

House at Church Street, Chelsea, London, by Eric Mendelsohn and Leife Chermayeff. Photograph from The Museum of Modern Art.

few public appearances. At a lecture in Dublin he deplored the senseless destruction of beauty and man's subjugation to the "brass band of metropolitan racket." Industrialization, he said, had enslaved men and added grime and noise to cities. The new world, he hoped, would bring a return to more natural ways of living where the machine would become a tool.

This lecture roused so much interest that Mendelsohn was asked to repeat it in Manchester, Sheffield, and Edinburgh. Another honor came to him when he was elected a fellow of the Royal Institute of British Architects.

In 1937, Mendelsohn again had to make the choice of a home. Long, frequent trips back and forth between England and Palestine left him unbearably tired. The bulk of his work was already being done in Palestine, and there seemed to be a good possibility that he would be appointed chief architect and planner for the Palestinian government. The prospect of having a part in building proud new cities excited him.

"You're in a position now to make a new contribution to a new society," Louise encouraged him.

Mendelsohn finally made the decision to live in Palestine, but when it came time to go it saddened him to leave his many English friends and their daughter. In Jerusalem, Louise and he made their home in a stone windmill with a domed timber roof. Eric's office was at the very top. There he worked on designs for the Hebrew University Agricultural College, the Trade School at Yaguri, and laboratories for the Weizmann Institute of Science and Daniel Wolff Pharmaceutical Institute—both at Rehoboth. His buildings were simple and less forbidding than those he had designed in Germany. He achieved elegance through proportion and made shadows serve him.

Mendelsohn had very little time away from architecture, but in his less hurried hours he wrote or worked in the garden with Louise. Soon after he moved to Palestine, one of his buildings, the Anglo-Palestine Bank in Jerusalem, begun two years before this, was completed. Tall glazed doors framed in white bronze opened from the vestibule into a majestic but serene hall that had a floor of quartzite with darker stripes of rose marble.

When war came to Europe in 1939, Mendelsohn tried to join the British army, but he was rejected because he was fifty-three and was not a native-born citizen. His urge to help found an outlet when refugees from persecution in Austria and Germany poured into Palestine. Among them were a number of Eric's friends and relatives. Louise's spirit of denial and self-sacrifice matched his own, but she did become alarmed when their funds dwindled. Because the war had halted all building activities, no money was coming in.

Reluctantly the Mendelsohns decided that once more they

would have to pull up stakes. On March 14, 1941, Louise and Eric voiced sad farewells to their friends who had gathered to see them off at the airport outside Jerusalem. Newspapers, in covering their departure, praised Mendelsohn's notable and varied contributions.

In Bombay, Indian architects honored Louise and Eric with a round of receptions and sight-seeing. The rest of the journey was made by boat. When Mendelsohn arrived in New York, the staff of *Architectural Forum* gave a welcoming party in his honor. Universities asked him to lecture. But he thought he should know the country and the language better before he lectured or built in it.

Louise understood Eric's need to learn more about the United States and they set forth on a tour of the country. Because they had limited funds, they camped out during much of the trip. Architect Albert Kahn entertained them in Detroit. At Taliesin they were guests of Frank Lloyd Wright. With his customary resilient adjustment to violent, abrupt changes, Mendelsohn was already looking ahead to the future.

At the end of the tour he settled down to writing, lecturing, and preparing an exhibit requested by the Museum of Modern Art. A few days after the exhibit opened, the country was shattered by news of the Japanese attack on Pearl Harbor. Although sick at heart, Mendelsohn went ahead with his lecture tour. At the University of California at Berkeley, he reviewed past failures in city planning. In the future, he said, there should be restrictions on the size of cities. Motor traffic must bypass congested areas.

This lecture and others were well received and later published, but they did not bring the income to which the Mendelsohns had become accustomed. Very little construction was going on, and the commissions went to native architects. Mendelsohn tried to increase his earnings through writing, but it was difficult for him to express himself in English. He took so much pains with each word that sometimes he spent a whole day formulating a sentence.

News of the war in Europe added to Mendelsohn's discouragement. Many of his relatives and friends were killed; others suffered persecution or exile. Only Louise's devotion and love kept him from a sense of utter futility.

Finances eased when the War Department made Mendelsohn an architectural consultant. He also obtained a Guggenheim fellowship. Some of his sketches drawn during this period were published in *Fortune* magazine.

During the final stage of the war, Mendelsohn looked hopefully upon the work being done by the San Francisco Conference working out the framework of the United Nations. Permanent peace was obtainable, he told lecture audiences, but both material and human resources must be used for the benefit of all men.

With the end of the war in sight, building projects again went forward. Mendelsohn was invited to St. Louis to discuss designs for a synagogue and community center for the B'nai Amoona Congregation.

They approved his plan for a structure modern in style but in keeping with Jewish traditions. To shield the temple from street noise, Mendelsohn placed it on an interior corner of the square of buildings. The roof of reinforced concrete had a parabolic shape. A large foyer connected the sanctuary and the assembly hall. Folding doors and hydraulically powered walls that would sink into slots made it possible to expand the seating capacity in either the sanctuary or the assembly hall.

Although almost fifty-nine, Mendelsohn was full of zest and eager to set up an office again. Of all the American cities he had seen, San Francisco appealed to him most. And architects Albert H. Hill and John Dinwiddie had invited him to become senior partner in their firm there. After a few months with Dinwiddie and Hill, he went into practice on his own.

Mendelsohn enjoyed life in San Francisco and no longer felt himself an alien after he took out citizenship papers. The apartment that he and Louise rented at the top of a private residence offered a view of the Bay that roused Eric's poetic bent. Inspired by the view, he wrote an occasional article and turned out endless designs.

His designs had great variety. Once, when a client asked him to repeat a house plan originally produced for someone else, Mendelsohn retorted, "Would you have asked Beethoven to go back to his seventh symphony when he was ready for his ninth?"

Occasionally Mendelsohn's ready wit and sharp tongue offended clients, but they always had the guarantee that he would give them an original and well-executed building. Even during the construction period, he would tear out a whole interior at his own expense if a door seemed an inch too far to one side.

The same concern for details was evident in his public buildings. For Maimonides Hospital in San Francisco, originally intended as a home for the chronically ill, he designed an eleven-story ward structure insulated from noisy slum streets by auxiliary buildings. The façade gave the impression of delicacy, even of gaiety. Balconies with white balustrades swung out in rhythmic curves and seemed almost to float in the air. Rooms were light, bright, and airy.

Mendelsohn turned from the hospital to several synagogues. This involved much travel, but he loved seeing the country and kept a diary sketchbook in which he wrote notes. He described California's redwoods as "God's own flagpoles."

He would become very excited when discussing synagogue plans with rabbis and their committees. "I couldn't sleep much last night," he would write to Louise. Sometimes he relayed comments about his clients such as, "Mrs. Rabbi doesn't like the bareness of the plan."

At the first meeting with a rabbi and his committee, Mendelsohn would ask many questions. "What is the program of your synagogue? How many children are there in the school. How traditional is your congregation?"

Then he would study the site intensively. In Cleveland, after a four-hour conference with Rabbi Cohen and his committee, Mendel-

125 □

sohn insisted on touring the thirty-acre site, although its trees and ravines were under snow.

That night he met with the committee again and sketched a tentative plan on a blackboard. They liked his idea for a circular temple on the hill between the ravines with the concrete dome resting on pillars enclosed by a band of glass. But they wanted stained glass windows. Mendelsohn thought stained glass inappropriate for this site.

The argument went on and on. Finally Mendelsohn said, "When you will show me the stained glass window that has upon it a design as beautiful as God's design of the surrounding trees and the sky above, then I will give you stained glass." He paused, then went on. "Didn't the Lord say, Let there be light? Why do you want to shut it out?"

Mendelsohn got his clear glass.

But he did not always make his point. In Washington, D.C., he lost a commission when a rabbi and his committee rejected the design he submitted as not dignified enough.

"I refuse to build a Greek temple," Mendelsohn told them.

Elsewhere, even after an initial design had been accepted, conflict might arise when his ideas met head-on with budgets, technical feasibility, availability of materials, or building needs.

After he had been given the go-ahead on a design, Mendelsohn would return home, usually by air, to redesign and refine. His first sketch had usually covered the essentials. From the rough preliminaries he had models prepared, then he worked from model to design then back to model, referring frequently to the first sketch, drawn in the heat of a consuming vision. Completed designs were always shared with Louise, who was a discerning but kindly critic.

The synagogues built in St. Louis, Cleveland, and other major cities were all militantly modern, but all were different, some had domes and others had soaring shafts. The buildings declared themselves boldly and had an exuberance about them, but they fitted gracefully with land or city scapes. For interiors, Mendelsohn tried to use textures, colors, and lines in a way that stirred emotional response and encouraged rediscovery of individual values.

Besides synagogues, Mendelsohn designed a radiation laboratory for the University of California at Berkeley and an electronics plant for Palo Alto, California. Houses included an L-shaped, four-level house built at Pacific Heights for Mr. and Mrs. Leon B. Russell. The main floor sheathed in redwood stood like a tray on legs and permitted a view of the bay. At one corner there was a cantilevered circular turret. The success of this and other homes led to a number of commissions. One young couple who had heard that Mendelsohn worked to music asked him to design a house for them according to Brahms.

Between designs, Mendelsohn sandwiched in teaching one day a week at the University of California School of Architecture. In his lectures he talked very little about technical aspects of construction, but when he did he drew interesting analogies. The expansion and contraction of steel and reinforced concrete, he said, was similar to the contraction and expansion of muscles. When a student asked if function was a primary element, Mendelsohn replied, "Yes, but function without sensibility remains mere construction. Visions are the vitamins necessary to the architect's artistic functions."

Always he tried to guide students to high achievements and constantly stressed the need for truth and for excellence in one's work and one's life. Once, when speaking of materials, he said, "It is cheating to do things with materials that contradict their nature."

Students had a deep respect and admiration for Mendelsohn. When he entered the drafting room, all conversation stopped immediately. Sometimes he would perch on a stool with students gathered around him and talk to them about sociology, people, building, personal creeds, and his own experiences as an architect. His wit, exuberance, and ability to dramatize held young potential architects spellbound. What he most wanted to do was to stretch the imagination of his students and to convey to them the importance and excitement of being an architect.

When Mendelsohn made the rounds to examine work assigned to his students, he carried a soft pencil. Sometimes he would pause at the drafting board of a promising pupil and his pencil would dance over the tracing paper as he made a suggestion. He detested imitation.

"Every flower is unique," he told his students. "Every snowflake is unlike every other one. It must be so with buildings, too."

Many individuals outside Mendelsohn's classes were exposed to his philosophy. In a lecture to a graduating class at the University of California, he said, "Many of you who sit here have talents far greater than mine, but few of you will fulfill your potential greatness, because you will quickly learn to compromise and settle for less than the best of which you are capable."

Mendelsohn himself never settled for less than his best. That best won awards. He was an honorary member of the International League of Modern Architecture, of the Arts Club of London, and of the Mexican Institute of Architects. One-man exhibitions of his works were held in many cities in many countries.

As Mendelsohn traveled about, lecturing or supervising projects, interviewers often sought him out. When one interviewer questioned him about his style, he replied, "I never wanted to create a style. I only wanted to create beauty." If asked about his hobbies, he usually answered, "Music, books, membership in the American Institute of Architects." But once he said, "I have my hands full just holding my visions, putting them on paper, and clarifying them."

Mendelsohn did indeed take very little time away from his work. Occasionally he and Louise went on a picnic or drove to Carmel. In 1952, they flew to Hawaii. Mendelsohn enjoyed the trip but found deeper satisfaction in home life than in travel. Louis and

Eric were delighted when their daughter Esther, who had been living in Europe, joined them. Later, she married a San Francisco surgeon, Dr. Peter Joseph. After Mendelsohn became a grandfather, he doted on his little granddaughter.

Toward the end of 1952, Mendelsohn began to feel almost unbearable pressure about his work. He had always said that he never needed outside pressure to drive him toward his goals because he was so fervently pressed from within. But now he felt overstimulated all the time and had trouble relaxing enough to get any sleep. He also had difficulty swallowing. Friction with clients increased.

As Christmastime neared, he longed for a period of solitude and rest. Louise, sensitive to his needs as always, insisted that she wanted to take a trip to New York by herself. But as soon as she was gone, he was terribly lonely. In one of a number of letters to her, he wrote, "To think of you, your understanding and your confidence, to know that you are there, is support and reward."

By the time Louise returned home, the swallowing condition had worsened. She insisted that he see a physician. On May 1 he underwent surgery for a tumor on the thyroid gland.

To Hans Schiller, an admirer and devoted friend, Mendelsohn confided, "Hans, I have just been told that I have but a short time to live. . . . There is still much to be done. I intend to continue to live and work as if nothing had happened."

And work he did. The visions that had always beckoned him toward something extraordinary grew brighter. He flew to Denver and to Baltimore on new projects.

But toward the end of August he became ill and was in and out of the hospital. Lying on a hospital bed, he asked Schiller to take notes on final plans for the interior of the Temple in St. Paul. He talked about the buildings he still meant to design. These remained only dreams. He died September 15, 1953.

In Germany, Palestine, England, and the United States, Mendelsohn left memorials to his artistry. He knew how to create beauty and give it majesty. His buildings pointed the way from the impersonal to the human.

Eric Mendelsohn left also the example of a life lived with imagination, enthusiasm, and inner consistency. Restraint and self-discipline controlled his fantasies.

"It is men like Mendelsohn who make humanity worth fighting for," said a student.

His poetic force, brilliance, and boundless energy inspired those who read or listened to his words. In tribute to his greatness of spirit, architect Irving D. Shapiro commented, "We who studied under Eric Mendelsohn have brushed with greatness."

SIX

RICHARD NEUTRA

Designer for Survival

When Richard Neutra was sixteen, his older brother William, a student of medicine, insisted that he see a physician who specialized in problems of vision. Mrs. Neutra went with him. After the examination, the doctor turned to Richard's mother and said, "Don't let him study architecture. It requires a lot of drawing. His eyes won't stand it in the long run." But the idea of not becoming an architect was unthinkable to Richard. He preferred to use his eyes for architecture while they lasted than to go into some other profession and save his vision.

Until the day Richard had the alarming report on his eyes, his life had been sheltered and happy. Born in Vienna, Austria, on April 8, 1892, he was the youngest son of a happy marriage. Samuel Neutra, who as a boy had been apprenticed to a metal caster and maker of cowbells, later became joint owner of a small factory that cast bronze and brass parts for the city of Vienna's gas and water

131 ☐

meters. Richard loved to visit his father's shop, where the employees obviously admired his father as he did.

His mother Elisabeth Glaser Neutra, youthful and lively, read him exciting stories and encouraged him in his projects. His sister Pepi stimulated him to paint. The Neutras were a close-knit family, and relatives came often to the apartment for food, talk, and music. Richard played the piano but liked better to listen to his brothers Siegfried and William play chamber music or sing songs like the one about a miner ready to die for mankind.

Richard first became conscious of architecture as such when he heard his brothers discussing whether the city hall was Romanesque or Gothic. But he had always been fascinated by designs—the claw legs of a table that looked like the claws of tigers in his picture books, the horse-chestnut leaves on the wallpaper in the Neutra apartment.

At the age of eight he was captivated by the subway stations designed by Otto Wagner. Many adult Viennese criticized Wagner as too modern, but to Richard he became Hercules, Buffalo Bill, and all the other heroes he had heard about rolled into one.

In high school, Richard did well in all his subjects but became interested in physiological psychology above all else. He was intrigued by ways in which it might be applied to architecture. Shouldn't designs for buildings be based on the physiological needs of those who lived in them? he asked himself and others.

Before Richard graduated from high school, his mother died. He had loved her deeply, and the loss made him feel unanchored and alone. Nothing worse could ever happen to him, he thought.

Arpad Weixlgaertner, his sister Pepi's suitor at the time, helped steer him away from his grief. A high court official, art historian, and director of the collection of bronzes at the Imperial Museum, Arpad gave Richard an appreciation of art and European culture and introduced him to prominent artists and musicians. Among them was the little-appreciated architect Adolf Loos.

When Loos saw that Richard was in earnest about architecture,

Richard Neutra

he invited him to spend several weeks in his drafting room to help on a project for a department store. Loos, an independent thinker, talked so much about the United States that Richard began to dream about going there himself. A much-admired portfolio of the work of Frank Lloyd Wright strengthened that desire.

After graduation from high school, Richard entered the Technische Hochschule in Vienna. One of his best friends was Ernst Freud, son of the famous psychologist Sigmund Freud. During a summer vacation they hiked through the Trieste area and the Dalmatian Islands. Richard carried a sketchbook in his knapsack, and in it he speedily painted the country through which they passed.

In 1914, a few months before he would have finished technical school, he was called into the army because of the uneasy international situation. Richard had already fulfilled his compulsory military service as a field artillery cadet and now ranked as an officer. He was placed in command of a mountain fortress on the southern frontier of the province of Hercegovina.

133 □

Part of Neutra's duty after war began was to defend roads that were lifelines for supplies. These must be kept passable no matter what the cost to lives. Neutra often rode horseback on his tours of inspection. Bullets fired by the enemy forces hiding in caves and crevices along the road frequently whistled past his ears. Much of the time he was hungry because the enemy had already seized or burned everything that was edible.

At Trebinje, Hercegovina, Neutra received his first commission as an architect and designed a teahouse. On a three-month leave in Vienna, he finished his work at the Technische Hochschule and graduated with high honors.

Back in service, Neutra contracted tropical malaria and for a year was sent from one hospital to another. He was in Trencin, Slovakia, when the Czech war of secession started. Eventually the Czech commander told him he could leave if he would go to Switzerland, a neutral country. Neutra's landlady, who had befriended him before this, gave him a letter of introduction to her cousin, who ran a rest home in Stäfa near Zürich.

At Sister Elsa's rest home, Neutra was enchanted by the glacier-studded mountains and the abundance of milk, ham, and eggs which he had not eaten for a long time. He was grateful to have escaped the war, but the only job he could find was a most low-salaried one at a landscape nursery in Zürich.

Neutra's supervisor Gustav Ammon sympathized with his wish to become an architect and taught Richard how to design plantings at sites of varied character. When Neutra's wages did not stretch far enough to replace the shabby Austrian uniform he had been wearing, he tried to economize on his lunches by taking slices of bread from the breakfast table with him when he left for work. At noon he ate them with roots, leaves, tomatoes, or dwarfed fruits growing on small trees in the nursery.

Through Sister Elsa, Neutra became acquainted with an elderly artist and writer, Alfred Niedermann. Homesick for his own family,

Neutra responded warmly to Niedermann's four grandchildren, who treated him as a brother. He soon fell in love with eighteen-year-old Dione, as attractive as she was gifted. Both as a cellist and vocalist she had professional skill. When she sang she played her own accompaniment on the piano.

By the time he was seriously in love with Dione, Neutra had a minor job with architects Wernli and Stäger at Wädenswil on the southern shore of the Lake of Zürich. He was glad to be designing again, but too much of his time went into building the fire and keeping it going, sweeping the office, and dusting drafting boards.

Neutra was depressed when the Niedermanns, who did not entirely approve of Dione's romance, sent her to Vienna. He made plans to go there to see his family and to help Dione celebrate her April birthday. If he could find an opening in an architectural office, he intended to stay on.

Richard had a happy homecoming. His sister Pepi had married Arpad Weilgaertner, and his beloved older brother Siegfried was now a patent attorney. His brother William had become a neurologist. Carefree hours with the family and Dione ended abruptly when Dione, Richard, and his father all became very ill with flu. Pepi cared for all of them in her own home, but for Samuel Neutra the illness was fatal.

His father's death hung over Richard like a dark bank of clouds. Desolation deepened when Dione returned to Switzerland. Uncertainty about his future plagued him. Conditions in postwar Vienna convinced him that it would be almost impossible to carve out a career there. What was he going to do? He was already twenty-eight and still only a rank beginner.

The age was a technical one, Neutra reasoned, as he tried to determine his next move. The country destined to play a major role for this age was the United States. From boyhood he had wanted to go there, but as an Austrian he would have difficulty gaining entry.

135 □

Neutra went ahead and got the required affidavit, but his visa was held up. Temporarily he served at a Friends' Mission. Then he accepted an invitation from his friend Ernst Freud to visit him in Berlin. For a short time he worked at a job he found there but then went on to a more interesting one offered to him by the Municipal Building Office in the small German town of Luckenwalde.

His major work was to design an extensive forest cemetery with building and landscaping. He also planned a settlement for low-income families being transplanted from cities to this semirural community. Neutra enjoyed his work and quickly made new friends with whom he hiked, bicycled, and sang in a glee club.

One day he saw color sketches of a factory that Eric Mendelsohn had submitted to the Luckenwalde building department. Neutra was so taken with the drawings that he went to Berlin to meet the architect.

The two men were drawn to one another immediately, and Mendelsohn offered him a good position. A few weeks after Neutra began work in the office he became a designer, and a short time later an officially credited collaborator on the *Berliner Tageblatt* Building.

While Mendelsohn was on a trip in Palestine, Neutra designed four exhibition houses for the Berlin suburb of Zehlendorf. The living rooms had revolving stages that could turn bays to supplement them. At the touch of a switch, a music, dining bay, or library moved into position next to the living room. These houses won much attention.

In 1922, Dione came to Berlin to study with the great cello teacher, Hugo Becker. Neutra yearned to marry her but could not yet offer her the kind of home she had a right to expect. That did not matter, Dione assured him. She wanted to be with him and help him.

After their marriage they moved into an improvised attic apartment in a suburb of Berlin. They had only a few furnishings. A bathtub in the basement served as a refrigerator. Dione, instead of complaining, looked for the good features such as the sound of the wind in the pines.

But Neutra was distressed when he thought of their future. Crippling inflation had beset the country still reeling from the impact of war. Prices rose a thousand per cent overnight. Then the welcome news came that Neutra and Mendelsohn had won first prize for the design they had submitted for the business center in Haifa, Palestine.

"We can use the money to make the new start in the United States which has beckoned for so long," he told Dione.

But by then she was expecting their first child.

"You go ahead and get located," she insisted. "I'll stay with my parents now and come as soon as I can."

Neutra could hardly bear the prospect of separation, but he was excited about the experiences he was sure awaited him in the new land. But opportunities were slow in opening up. Partly because of his nationality and inadequate English, the only job he could find was a minor one in Manhattan. The room he rented for two dollars a week had a bed in it but not much else. He missed Dione terribly and longed to see their baby, named Frank out of admiration for Frank Lloyd Wright.

Tired of drawing Gothic ornaments, Neutra decided he might do better in Chicago. He got there on a raw, gray day in November, 1923. Because he had been told that immigrants were welcome at Hull House, he asked directions and then trudged off, carrying his bags. The founder Jane Addams greeted him with heart-warming cordiality.

As soon as Neutra had unpacked, the thing he most wanted to do was to see Frank Lloyd Wright's prairie houses, which he had studied with so much devotion. Neutra had visualized the houses standing on prairies and was surprised to find them in the city itself. It startled him to see the buildings in a run-down condition and the owners less than appreciative.

Afterward Neutra also visited the buildings of Louis Sullivan.

When he went to pay tribute to their builder, he was shocked to find him ill and living in poverty in a dreary tenement room.

"I have been forgotten," Sullivan told him.

"This is not true," Neutra protested. "Your fame and influence are world-wide. Since I was a young man in Vienna I have heard your name and admired you. And now I am here."

As he left Sullivan's room, Neutra was dejected. Wright's run-down houses, the way the press flayed him, the neglect of Sullivan made him feel as if he had arrived in a fairyland from which the fairies had fled.

"I am desperate to see you," he wrote Dione.

Dione wrote back that she could get a passport to come as a musician, but this would mean leaving little Frank behind. She would, however, keep trying to get a passport that would permit the baby's entry.

Meanwhile Neutra taught a class in drafting at Hull House and worked as a draftsman in the firm of Holabird and Roche. At the time, the office was designing the new 2,400-room Palmer House. Because Neutra wanted to become acquainted with American techniques, he did not reveal his previous architectural and artistic experience.

His good work on the technical problems assigned him and his ability to speak French with Pellini, director of design for the firm, led to a promotion. He became a liaison officer between designers and all departments.

Neutra now commuted back and forth between his job and a home in Highland Park. To pass the time, he began preparing notes for a book he hoped to write on American building techniques. In odd moments he took pictures that might be useful in illustrating it. But these activities did not prevent loneliness. He wrote Dione to come alone, if she must, but to come.

Chicago, his job, everything looked rosier after she got there, but both Dione and he ached to have their baby with them. Finally they were able to make arrangements for Dione's mother to come and bring little Frank.

One expectation was still unfulfilled—Neutra had not yet met Frank Lloyd Wright. He saw him for the first time at Graceland Cemetery at Louis Sullivan's funeral in April, 1924. After the service, Neutra went up to Wright and in a halting voice told him what his work had meant to him. Wright insisted on taking him out for dinner and afterward invited the whole Neutra family to Taliesin. The visit led to a friendship.

Neutra's association with Mendelsohn and Wright and his practical experiences at Holabird and Roche had given him a stockpile of skills and ideas. He was eager to set up his own office. The mild climate of California appealed to him. There would be no icy storms there to balk a builder. And Westerners were more footloose, less bound by tradition. Neutra hoped that this would mean that Californians would respond with enthusiasm to new trends in architecture.

Shortly after the birth of their second son, Dion, the Neutras moved to Los Angeles. Richard was disappointed when he found no opening either as an architect or as a teacher. It was a trial to him to be bursting with stored-up creativity and have no chance to use it. His career had already been delayed by war, the general poverty following the war, and a move to a foreign land.

While he waited, longing for tasks to master, Neutra helped John Entenza to launch the magazine *Arts and Architecture*. He also spent much time at the Academy of Modern Art, quartered in an old house. Students began seeking him out. To them he revealed many of his ideas about what had to be done before designs were put on paper.

The architect, he said, should think first about who would live in the house. People were assailed by a complexity of shapes, colors, smells, noises. It was up to the architect to find out how clients re-

139 □

sponded to these. He should also sense the muscular, nervous, and emotional strains that beset the individuals when alone and when surrounded.

There was, Neutra insisted, a relationship between houses and health. Bad housing could breed tension, irritation, fatigue. He challenged young architects to create buildings that would reduce stresses and mental friction.

"Through the kind of house you provide," he told students, "you can become the evil demon or the protective angel of a family."

During his first months in California, Neutra finished the book he had begun as notes jotted down on a commuter's train in Chicago. Titled *Wie baut Amerika*, "How America Builds," the book was published in Stuttgart in 1926. In it Neutra had outlined in detail the steps taken in construction of big buildings and illustrated them with effective photographs taken with his own cheap camera. The book became a best seller, and his publisher asked for another. Neutra then began preparation of a manuscript that would deal with the work of architectural pioneers like Louis Sullivan.

But some clients had begun to come to Neutra's office, and since he took their trust very seriously he had less time for writing. Neutra was very enthusiastic when naturopath Dr. Philip N. Lovell most unexpectedly asked him to design a home for a Los Angeles site that had Griffith Park hills as a backdrop. The faraway ocean was visible over the trees in the foreground.

Neutra and Dr. Lovell paid so much attention to biological features in their planning of the home that it seemed right to call it the "Health House." Neutra planned a steel framework with walls of thin air-compressed concrete, expanses of glass, and cantilevered sun decks overlooking the hillside.

Because the steel skeleton was to have largely prefabricated sections, it would have to be preassembled. This meant that Neutra had to work out measurements to an eighth-of-an-inch exactness. He was so keyed up during the designing period that he often got up at four in the morning to work on the plans. During the construction period in the shop, he supervised each step.

Health House had been an exhausting assignment, thought Neutra, on the day he stood watching painters put finishing touches on the interior. At that moment he smelled smoke. When he rushed to the telephone to call the fire department, he could think only of the woods surrounding the house, the inflammable oils, and the old newspapers piled all over by the painters.

While Neutra waited for the firemen, the sky turned black with smoke. The blaze advanced like a roaring hurricane. It appeared that all his work had been for nothing. But just at the moment the conflagration reached the Lovells' boundary line, the fire department came. Health House stood, but it was surrounded by a wasteland of gray ashes.

Nevertheless the house created a stir. Many thousands came to see it. The New York Museum of Science and Industry asked for a steel model. His had been no dizzy success story, Neutra told reporters. And he regretted that publicity on the house made him appear more an engineering wizard than an architect primarily interested in the art of knowing man and giving him the right surroundings.

During the time he had been designing private homes and apartments, Neutra had also been working on a project he called "Rush City Reformed"—a layout for a model metropolis of one million population. He believed that in the deserts of man-made cities there should be order and little oases. These he achieved by grouping and orienting apartment, row, and patio houses around unfenced common parks. Downtown, entire ground floors beneath stilted buildings would be given over to rolling traffic and parking. Pedestrians would take elevators to walks at second- or third-story level where they could enter shops above traffic.

Freeways, express trains, airports—all forms of transportation in Rush City Reformed would be ingeniously interlinked. Multilevel railway stations would have heliports on top. In residential areas there would be pleasant pedestrian lanes separated from roadways. Heavy traffic would have to pass around and along the edge of a neighborhood.

Rush City Reformed became a favorite topic in the class that Neutra taught at the Academy of Modern Art. Student discussions and zestful participation in projects helped him to jell his own thoughts. Neutra also had much to say about the use of materials.

"The most significant material which the architect handles," he told his students, "is human minds—not sticks, stone, and hardware."

He urged them to cherish and understand human nature. They should allay anxiety and try to fulfill the dreams of their clients instead of indulging in willful self-expression. A client, he told his students, might have scraped together all his savings or strained his credit to pay for a home, and the architect must not disappoint him by failure to meet his needs, aspirations, or hopes. Courtesy, compassion, integrity, and patience were qualities an architect needed in dealing with clients.

"Know man and love him, if you want to serve him," he admonished.

Teaching, writing, designing had left Neutra terribly tired. What he most wanted to do in 1929 was to take Dione and the children and go to Europe for a vacation among relatives and friends. But now he was in much demand and had lectures scheduled in Japan. Because Dione insisted that he wouldn't get any rest at all if the family went with him, they decided that Neutra would go to Japan alone and then travel by sea to Europe. Meanwhile Dione and the children would take a freighter through the Panama Canal and meet him in England.

On the boat to Japan, Neutra was so tired that he wondered if he would ever be able to go forward with his career. Yokohama was bleak the morning he landed, but the Japanese surrounded him with friendliness and crowded into lecture halls to hear him. A Japanese publisher brought out a compilation of his designs.

From Japan, Neutra traveled to Hong Kong, the Portuguese colony of Macao, Kwangtung, China, and then on through the Indian Ocean. He was extremely lonely for his family. He had never ceased being amazed at the way Dione kept alive her creative gifts and yet managed to be a wonderful wife and mother. The linkage of their lives had been joyous and right.

In Europe, Neutra relaxed for a brief time with his relatives and lovingly introduced Dione and the children to colleagues and friends. He visited the Bauhaus as an invited guest of Mies van der Rohe, attended a meeting of the International Congress of Modern Building in Brussels, and spoke in Frankfurt and Cologne.

Speeches made in Zürich and Basel, Switzerland, called Neutra to the attention of the millionaire Dutch industrialist Cornelius van der Leeuw, who invited Neutra and his family to visit him in his home in Rotterdam.

While there, Neutra met many leaders in the field of architecture. One of these men asked whether science and technology would ever replace the art of design. Neutra did not think they would. Technology and science, he said, could aid but never supplant art. The architect must always rely on initiative and insight to a degree.

Although preoccupied with architecture, Neutra found science fascinating. Science, he said, had sometimes been indifferent to personal needs and moral values. But now it had begun to recognize biological individuality.

As the time neared for Neutra to return home, Dione suggested that she and the children stay in Europe for a time to see if Sigmund Freud could help Frank. An injury at birth had left an impairment in the speech center of their lovely son, and the condition had become worse.

The idea of having to live even temporarily without his family dismayed Neutra. He toyed with the idea of practicing architecture in Europe, but he was now a naturalized citizen of the United States, and it seemed best to return to the country he loved.

Back in New York, Neutra lectured at the New School for Social Research. At the invitation of the Aluminum Company of America (Alcoa), he went to Cleveland to redesign the "Pullmans of the Highway" of the White Motor Company. After his design was happily accepted he traveled to Chicago to lecture at the Art Institute, where he introduced the idea of a Bauhaus in this country. Afterward he returned to California, but he felt rootless and downcast without his family.

A month after he reopened an office, Cornelius Van der Leeuw came to visit him. Neutra, driving his old Chevrolet, took him to see Health House.

Van der Leeuw was most enthusiastic. "Why don't you build one for yourself?" he asked.

"I have not the funds," Neutra told him.

Leeuw wanted to finance him outright, but Neutra felt he could not accept such a generous gift. He did, however, yield to the Dutchman's persuasiveness to the extent of accepting a loan which he expected to repay with three per cent interest.

Dione was excited about the plans for the house when she came from Europe with the children, but Neutra kept delaying the building of it because he wanted it to be just right. He had already realized that, in the future, the population explosion would severely limit space. He wanted to prove with his own house that privacy is possible even in cramped quarters.

For a site, Neutra chose a lot sixty by seventy feet in the middle of Los Angeles. The property faced lovely Silver Lake. He designed a long narrow house in two sections, joined at ground level by a closed-in patio and a connecting wing. Each unit had its own living room and kitchenette. In his office complex, Neutra had two large drafting rooms, a storage room, a small reception room, a secretarial office, and a study.

Throughout the house, strategically placed mirrors gave an air of spaciousness. Neutra utilized novel materials and unusual devices such as electronically controlled glass panels that made the informal garden living room part of the patio. Reflection of outside illumination assured privacy behind the plate-glass front. Shrubs and trees screened the dwelling from the neighbors. In the upper living quarter, folding doors opened onto a porch overlooking Silver Lake.

This home, which he called the V.D.L. Research House in honor of Van der Leeuw, won praise for its flexibility and the way it fused with the site. Neutra knew he had achieved what he desired when architects predicted that this home would be immune to obsolescence.

During the 1930's Neutra built a number of other houses and constantly experimented with new ideas. He had patents for chair-spring supports, prefabricated footings, and a table that could be raised from a low occasional table to a dining table. The William Beard House at Altadena used radiant heat installations in the hollow floors and walls of sheet steel. The depression of the 1930's spurred him into research on prefabrication. He believed that the use of prefabricated parts was sound, logical, and economical, but that there must be individuality.

In 1933, Neutra won first prize in the *House Beautiful* competition for the house he built for actress Anna Sten. An all-steel house entered in a *Better Homes in America* competition won the magazine's gold medal award. Inspired by Neutra's ideas, *Better Homes and Gardens*, usually a conservative magazine, published designs of his houses and carried an article in which he discussed houses of the future.

Although Neutra liked building houses, schools were his great love. He contended that a living-room atmosphere in classrooms made children more ready to learn. When he was commissioned to do an elementary school in Los Angeles, he broke the tradition of two or more stories. His one-story building was only one classroom deep, with a glass front on one side and elevated strip windows on the other. Electronically operated doors opened the glass front onto the patio. There were no fixed seats.

Because his plan was so daring compared to the standard elementary buildings of the 1930's, the school board placed his school in an outlying district on Corona Avenue. Neutra might not have had the chance to build even then had not the school principal, Nora Sterry, stood up for his novel plan and the League of Women Voters helped sway the Board of Education.

The Corona School, when completed, won the honor award of the Pittsburgh Glass Competition and received national attention. In time, Neutra had requests to design other schools, including Emerson Junior High School in West Los Angeles and the California Military Academy, in which he used some prefabricated parts and sections of sheet steel.

Among the dozens of projects in which Neutra was involved were several commissioned by the United States government. He planned residence centers for the National Housing Authority and housing developments that included six hundred homes in the Channel Heights area at San Pedro for wartime shipyard employees. There Neutra had to work with a site deeply cut by canyons. Instead of going in and bulldozing the land, he carefully fitted houses to its contours; all had garden space and a view of the ocean. The praise that this project earned meant more to Neutra because his son Dion had worked so devotedly with him.

At about the same time, Neutra won an honor award in the Hall of Fame at the New York World's Fair, the honor award of the Republic of Uraguay, and an honor award from *House and Garden*.

Shortages of materials during World War II left Neutra undaunted. The architect, he said, could be influenced by materials he did *not* have as well as by materials he *did* have. In proof of this he designed the Nesbitt House, using redwood board and batten,

Corona School, Los Angeles, California, by Richard Neutra. Julius Shulman photograph.

common brick, and glass, and achieved a new combination of transparency. The Kelton Apartments received an A.I.A. award.

In 1944, Neutra became chairman of the California State Planning Board, on which he had served for several years. As World War II drew to a close, he went to Puerto Rico as consultant on a fifty-million-dollar long-range building program designed to raise health and educational standards on the island.

This project appealed to him because he had longed to see the gap bridged between industrial strongholds like the United States and struggling peoples. Architects, he felt, must not think solely in terms of chrome and steel for Fifth Avenue. They must meet the needs of people everywhere. For Puerto Rico, Neutra designed 150 schools and 128 health and community centers—some of these could be duplicated by unskilled peasants.

He welcomed opportunities for experimentation. The desert, he believed, would become an important spill-over region when the population increased and so was very enthusiastic when Easterner Edgar Kaufmann asked him to design a desert hideaway at Palm Springs, California. The flat, pavilionlike house was linked to the terrain with boulders and plants native to the region. The four courtyards and walls and floors were piped for summer cooling and winter heating. In architectural interest, the desert home equaled Kaufmann's Falling Water House in the East designed by Frank Lloyd Wright.

For the Warren Tremaine House at Montecito in Santa Barbara County, California, Neutra used reinforced concrete. The plan permitted domestic living to expand outdoors. The Tremaine House won architectural awards, as had the home built for the Kaufmanns, and the architectural critic Sigfried Giedion gave it his highest praise.

The Moore House in the hot, dry Ojai Valley in California had a hovering roof and a terrace jutting out into a cooling pond or pool. Stone stairs and a vine-covered pergola connected the main house and guest apartment. The Hall residence at Newport Beach,

Desert House by Richard Neutra. Photograph by Julius Shulman.

California, built as a house for yachtsmen, had a maritime character and opened toward a private pier.

For all these homes Neutra had operated on a generous budget. But he also continued to build homes for which he received only a very small commission. He worked as best he could with all who came. "An architect who seeks and selects only easy clients is like a missionary who deals only with selected heathens," he told Dione.

Neutra put just as much heart into a modest house as an expensive one. While working with clients he developed a deep, warm relationship. Those who gave trouble—worriers, rebels, head-shakers —were rare and usually were convinced in the end.

One client, however, kept asking for revisions and then in the end rejected the changes she herself had made and said that she hated the house. Even though the client's discontent was her own, Neutra was unhappy. Letters from others, telling him how they loved the homes he had built for them, helped offset the one failure.

Most of Neutra's houses were one-story, sensitively proportioned, compact structures with expanses of glass. Large sliding doors made patios part of the real-use area. Redwood, used out of necessity at first, became a favorite material.

Because of his careful workmanship, Neutra's houses were both economical and durable. When he had first started practicing in California, bankers had often refused to give loans on houses he designed, arguing that they were too unusual. But now home owners found the architect's name an asset when getting a loan or selling their property. His Zürich nursery experiences served him well when it came to landscaping. Outside as well as inside he perfected the tiniest details.

Neutra would have preferred to continue to design schools or houses with green things growing around them. But he realized that a mobile, expanding population and a decrease in available land would make apartment houses a necessity.

To handle requests for apartments and other large-scale projects, Neutra felt the need of a partner. Perhaps, he told himself, lone-wolf careers were becoming less possible, less necessary, less desirable.

Robert E. Alexander, architect and city planner, responded with enthusiasm when Neutra suggested that they organize a firm. Their offices on Glendale Boulevard, which Richard built with his son Dion, overlooked a landscaped garden. Neutra set up highly organized, dovetailed planning procedures. Because an inspiration often came to him at night, he had a telephone and intercom system at his bedside at home. It was not at all unusual for him to call a secretary or staff member who had been assigned to night duty and discuss a plan or dictate a convincing letter to a client.

One of the major undertakings of the firm was a redevelopment plan for Sacramento, California. Two of its main features were: distributed rather than centralized parking for cars, and reclamation of a blighted area along the river front. Neutra paved the way for acceptance of the project by working step by step through all possible civic organizations and ethnic groups.

Involved as he was in civic projects and building plans, Neutra never neglected his family, which had been expanded by the birth of Raymond Richard. Music was a favorite pastime. Dione often sang old ballads and folk songs collected from many countries. With artistic ingenuity and finesse she had arranged these so she could accompany herself on cello or piano. When Dione was a featured artist at some public performance, Neutra was an enthusiastic admirer.

Dione shared his triumphs, but she also helped him find courage when projects collapsed. At one time Neutra planned a center for 3,400 families in an area adjacent to Elysian Park in Los Angeles. After he had worked out the last detail, the City Council and Housing Authority canceled the project.

But Neutra and his partnership had no dearth of commissions and designed a number of California schools—Kester Elementary

School in Los Angeles, Alamitos Intermediate School at Garden Grove, a high school in Palos Verdes, the Elementary Training School for the University of California at Los Angeles, and two Observation Nursery Schools in Los Angeles. An unusual feature of this kind of school was an observation area enclosed by polaroid glass. Teachers and administrators could, without being seen, watch the children and record their impressions. The ring-plan school built for the Lemoore Naval Air Station in central California introduced a plan much imitated by other architects. The one-story building with detached classrooms and patio areas was ranged around a usable green area. The Board of Education named it the Richard J. Neutra School in recognition of the architect's innovations. They also referred to him as a "patron of education by environment."

Other buildings appeared on many college campuses—at the University of Nevada, San Fernando Valley (California) State College, and St. John's College in Annapolis, Maryland. At the Living Library and Communicative Arts Center for Adelphi College in New York City, he designed a time-space gate consisting of a translucent globe depicting the earth where one could see places in the news pinpointed and keyed into a continuously operating news ticker. Current news was projected on various screens.

While he carried out his numerous building programs, Neutra was continuously surrounded by apprentices from many parts of the United States and foreign countries. To him it seemed a privilege to stimulate younger men to carry on their profession and their daily lives with high ideals. When he lectured he was never sure that students had gained anything. They learned most, he felt, when they saw him suffer at his daily work.

Neutra encouraged apprentices to be systematic about their files and records, and also about their thoughts. "Architecture is an ordered craft—like playing a violin," he told them. An office required as much mental teamwork as a football team or a chamber music group. This same teamwork extended to the many persons they would work with on a building—workmen, engineers, contractors. Confidence of co-workers and clients, he said, could be won through systematics and lost through confusion. Confidence could also be lost through misdemeanors, oversights, neglect.

The confidence Neutra himself inspired led to widely scattered projects. He crisscrossed the United States, lecturing, acting as consultant on city planning, supervising building.

With his son Dion and partner Robert Alexander he collaborated on a ten-year master plan for the island and port of Guam. Neutra had always been interested in ports, which in his mind were associated with glitter and excitement. It troubled him that so many of them had become filthy places, both physically and morally. In Shanghai, he had seen starving coolies with singsong voices carry backbreaking loads to their little boats. The ports he designed in Guam and elsewhere were functional but far from drab.

In Spain, he and Dion captained forty architects who worked practically around the clock to develop houses, schools, clubs, churches, business centers, and neighborhood projects for United States Air Force personnel stationed there.

Plans for ports, islands, and buildings brought a steady flow of awards. In the Southern California A.I.A. Competition, Neutra won the honor award for the best residence in three years. He received honor awards from *House and Garden* competition and from *Progressive Architecture* competition. An issue of *L'Architecture d'Aujourd'hui* was devoted almost entirely to Neutra, and an issue of *Time* magazine in 1949 with an article on his career had a portrait of him on the cover with the caption, "What will the neighbors think?" Neutra was the first architect to receive cover notice on this magazine.

In the United States during the 1950's, Neutra's buildings, mostly elaborated in collaboration with the staff of the partnership, were nearly all devoted to community needs—schools, chapels, churches, libraries, hospitals, hotels, clubs, museums. He designed

153 □

hospitals in India and Puerto Rico, a sanatorium in Italy, and a theater in Düsseldorf, Germany, that won the highest award in an international competition.

Busy as he was, Neutra somehow found time to write two hundred or more articles and several books that became known throughout the world. His three-volume *Buildings and Projects* is a pictorial as well as verbal summary of his achievements. In *Mystery and Realities of the Site* he flays land developers who "cut the trees, excavate the good earth, bulldoze and bully the landscape . . . blow up the natural habitat of bird and beast."

Life and Human Habitat, a handsome album of his architecture, has unusual pictures side by side with thoughts, philosophy, and physiological psychology. In *Survival through Design,* Neutra sets forth the idea that design is a survival aid because good housing for all of life's activities relieves irritation and thus contributes to calmness and health.

But words never interrupted the output of buildings. Among these were Offices and Auditorium for the Amalgamated Clothing Workers, the United Auto Workers' Building, the Northwestern Insurance Building, and the Hall of Records—all in Los Angeles.

Outstanding clubhouses and hotels built in California during this period were Eagle Rock Playground Club House, the San Pedro Community Hotel near Los Angeles, and Holiday House at Malibu Beach. In the last-named, each apartment could be entered from its own landscaped, covered walk, and each living and sleeping room offered a view of the Pacific.

Between bursts of design Neutra traveled a great deal to fulfill the demands of his profession. He lectured in Asia, Canada, South America, and Mexico, where he was guest of honor of Mexico City. He served as adviser to the governments of Turkey and Kenya, to the mayor of South Africa, and to the president of Venezuela, and was guest of the All India Planning Commission.

Wherever he went, warm-hearted, attractive Dione was at his

side. She was a natural linguist and entered freely into the life of alien cultures. In Santo Domingo, Paris, or Cuzco she won the hearts of groups of street urchins by singing to them. She was received with equal enthusiasm when she preceded Richard, as she often did, in a musical program before one of his lectures or at a reception.

Whether the Neutras were in Guam, Spain, Africa, or India, Richard used spare moments for sketching. Aboard airplanes, ships, trains, or in cars, if officials or clients stopped long enough for him to get out his sketch pad, his pencil was busy.

Baltic shore lines with scraggly pines, ceiba trees on the Congo, monasteries, Burmese temples, native huts, medieval castles became his subjects. He drew pictures of Gauchos in Argentina, of bull-fighters and dancers with whirling skirts in Seville. Hundreds of these emotion-provoking sketches appeared later in special collections.

At home once more after his global lectures, Neutra would be overwhelmed by the work confronting him, but he approached each project with enthusiasm. Every building was different, and to evaluate the client's requirement list, gain his confidence, and crystallize the design, he felt to be the most creative effort of the architect.

Neutra was excited when the Gemological Institute of America, a nonprofit organization, asked him to design a research center for jewelers. He liked the idea of housing for men who, in a land threatened by mechanization, still relied on skillful fingers and trained eyes. Flexible arrangement of the interior permitted conversion of classrooms into lecture halls and extensions of laboratories for gem testing. A free-swinging patio stairway lent eye appeal.

One of the most striking structures Neutra and Alexander designed for religious purposes was Miramar Chapel at La Jolla, California. At Santa Ana, California, they built a neatly tailored police headquarters that had pivoted louvers; electronically controlled, the louvers compensated in steady slow motion for the rotation of the earth and kept glaring sun outside.

Neutra's essential dedication through the years had been to find

a reliable physiological basis for design, and so he was very interested in medical and scientific buildings. He believed that pleasant surroundings encourage persons who are ill and help them to relax. For this reason he built the San Bernardino (California) Medical Center around a large patio visible from the inside of the buildings through large glass areas.

During construction of this and other buildings, Neutra did everything possible to spark his collaborators with enthusiasm and to enlist cooperation of workmen at the site. He had a warm sympathy for the men who perched on swinging scaffolds and worked in cramped positions.

Even with so many buildings demanding his attention, Neutra found time to lecture in many cities in the United States. One of the joys of his jaunts about the country was seeing his architectural friends—Mies van der Rohe, Gropius, Mendelsohn, Saarinen, Stone. After one of his appearances, a reporter described him as a "distinguished-looking, owl-beaked dynamo who preaches the gospel of modern architecture."

But he did more than preach architecture; he spoke always of values. "Man is the real subject of architecture," he told young architects at Yale, Carnegie Tech, Texas A. and M., Montana, Washington, and Utah universities, and many others. In speeches to the general public, he hammered away at the necessity for removal of parasitic slums. People had a right, he said, to live in decent houses. The dreams they had for such havens could not be left stunted.

At the invitation of the University of Arizona, Neutra went to Tucson to give the keynote address for an industrial workshop attended by governors and mayors. While he was there with Dione, John Riddick of the Tucson *Daily Citizen* invited the Neutras to travel to the Mexican border with him. Out on a stretch of arid wasteland, Neutra remembered that he had been asked to call a Washington, D.C., number when he had a moment.

157 □

Northwestern Insurance Co. Building, Los Angeles, California. Photograph by Julius Shulman.

At the home of a rancher he put through the call and learned that he had been selected to design the Lincoln Memorial Museum on Cemetery Ridge at Gettysburg. The idea of creating a museum that would become a shrine for the free world exhilarated Neutra. This was only one in a series of laurels that had been coming his way, but he still had not become accustomed to having garlands heaped upon him. A fellow of the American Institute of Architects, he had carried off many honor awards. He had been named an honorary member of the Royal Institute of British Architects, the Colombia Association of Architects, the East Indian African Institute of Architects, and other distinguished groups.

Neutra garnered many gold medals and well over fifty prizes in national and international competitions for commercial and residential designs. The Technical University of Berlin and other universities bestowed honorary degrees. Columbia University awarded him a silver medallion. Venice made him honorary member of the College of Academicians of Fine Arts. The Federal Republic of Germany gave Neutra its Highest Order of Merit, and the Buenos Aires Society of Architects, as well as that of the Congo, elected him honorary president.

As recognition came his way, Neutra constantly expressed gratitude for persons and situations he readily credited with having encouraged and stimulated him. A most important factor had been his marriage to Dione, a faithful and harmonious partner. But he also had been fortunate, he felt, to grow up in Vienna, with its background of culture and internationalism. After he received the Grand Prize of the City of Vienna, he commented, "I feel strangely at home in Manila, or Lima, or Madrid. A local boy of Vienna cannot help being a sort of cosmopolitan boy."

In the years since that boyhood in Vienna, Neutra had done as much as anyone to prove that glass, steel, and concrete can be used inventively. The explanation for that inventiveness, he thought, lay in his respect for man, "the most priceless material in the world."

During the 1960's Neutra was busy with large residences at home and abroad—housing communities near Hamburg and Frankfurt, office buildings and universities in Pakistan and elsewhere. The United States Embassy in Karachi, Pakistan, faced the largest green area in the city. It had water basins at the front and rear and large warehouses for economic aid supplies.

Neutra's publications during these years included *World and Dwelling* and *Life and Shape,* which explores the fascinating subject of shape but is also biographical.

A new round of honors included a trip to Brazil as guest of the President of Brazil in the nation's new capital city, Brasilia, on which Neutra had been asked to confer. Several residences and Miramar Chapel received A.I.A. merit awards. The American Institute of Steel Construction presented him an award of excellence for the Garden Grove Community Church. And he gained membership in the National Institute of Arts and Letters and the National Academy of Design.

As a tribute to Neutra, friends and patrons founded the Richard J. Neutra Institute, with offices in Los Angeles and European cities, to further the kind of research he had inspired and to disseminate his findings. Studies were envisioned on the impacts of environment, emotion, and the organic make-up on man. Founders planned to sponsor lectures and seminars, publish articles and books, and establish a library based on Neutra's books, research, speeches, reports, and exhibits.

The period during which Neutra was receiving honors also brought some reverses. In 1963 the V.D.L. house burned, but it was reconstructed the following year.

More than ever, Neutra took pleasure in his family, including his grandsons Gregory and Nicholas. It was a deep satisfaction to him to have Dion as a collaborator and to see his son Raymond Richard going forward with plans to become a doctor.

Neutra's effect on the architecture of our time has been profound and far-reaching. His office buildings, schools, auditoriums, judicial facilities, health centers, housing developments, mansions, and modest homes line Pacific shores, dot tropical islands, sit at the feet of virgin peaks in Switzerland.

Many features of his schools have become standard, and his versatile, original houses and public buildings have been widely pondered. Architects Egon Winkens, John Blanton, Raphael Soriano, Harwell Harris, and others have adopted his architectural styles. Neutra's writings, his faithful followers, and the Institute set up in his name insure that what his dedication has wrought will continue beyond the span of his own life.

Because his interest lay more in people than in planks and plywood, Neutra exerted an influence beyond his profession of architecture. "Being faithful to oneself is important," he told his apprentices. "It perhaps teaches one to remain faithful to others." Richard J. Neutra's faithfulness has been clearly expressed in his life as well as in his buildings.

SEVEN

EDWARD DURELL STONE

Campaigner for Permanence and Beauty

Edward D. Stone won his first architectural award at the age of fourteen when he designed a birdhouse for a contest sponsored by the local lumberyard and the Fayetteville, Arkansas, *Daily Democrat*. To make the outside look like a log cabin, he surfaced it with sassafras branches cut in half. Ed was elated when he won a two-and-a-half-dollar prize for something that had been fun to do.

He had always liked to draw and build boats and miniature towns in the room where he had his own carpentry shop. But he had no driving ambition to become an architect. Career plans could wait. For now he was much more interested in joining schoolmates or his father to swim, fish, or hunt arrowheads. Ed's relaxed attitudes had been encouraged by the easy-going life in his home and in the community of Fayetteville, where he had been born in 1902.

Benjamin Stone, formerly a merchant, now managed the property he had inherited from Ed's grandfather Stephen Stone, a founder of the community. An avid reader, he was an authority on almost any subject. He also set a pattern of justice and uprightness.

"Never say anything about anyone unless you can say something good," he told Edward and his brother Hicks.

Ruth Johnson Stone had come to Fayetteville from St. Louis to teach English in the University of Arkansas. Talented in the arts, she encouraged Edward in his artistic tendencies. The Stones had a deep affection for one another, and their home life was pleasant and unruffled.

When Edward was sixteen his whole world changed. His father had become land-poor and had to sell most of his property to get money to pay taxes. But to Ed this loss was slight compared to the death of his mother, to whom he had been devoted.

When he entered the University of Arkansas a short time later, he had not settled on a major, although he took a number of courses in art. Among fellow students, his ability as a storyteller and cartoonist and his genuine interest in others made him immensely popular.

The summer Ed was eighteen and a six-footer, his brother invited him to spend the summer vacation with him in Boston. Hicks, fourteen years older, was now an established architect.

Ed found a job with an electrical appliance company. Evenings and weekends he and Hicks often walked around, studying buildings in Boston, Salem, or Marblehead.

"If you want to be an architect," Hicks told him, "you've got to love buildings more than anything else in the world, and you've got to work hard."

Exposure to good architecture and to Hick's enthusiasm convinced Ed that he wanted to have a career in that profession. He returned to his studies with more ambition than he had ever experienced before. But the University of Arkansas had no school of architecture. After he had taken freehand and mechanical drawing courses, Ed decided to go back to Boston.

Edward D. Stone

There he got a job as office boy in the firm of Strickland, Blodgett, and Law and enrolled for night courses at the Boston Architectural Club. To put an idea for a building down on paper and see it take form was a wonderful experience for him. Sometimes he would become so excited that he would stay up all night sketching. The visiting professors who came from Harvard and the Massachusetts Institute of Technology praised his designs highly.

One night, Henry R. Shepley, who headed a top-notch architectural firm, came to the club. He stood for several moments, looking at one of Ed's drawings.

"You have turned a commonplace design into a thing of beauty," Shepley told him. He also offered him a position as draftsman in his firm.

While he was working at Shepley's office, Ed was awarded a scholarship to Harvard on the basis of a design submitted in a competition. At Harvard he led an active social life, but he also

163 □

worked hard. He spent much of his free time with Hicks, who added to his architectural education.

"There are two attitudes you must bring to your profession," Hicks told him, "singleness of purpose and an open mind. The first comes easily to a person with energy and ambition. Keeping an open mind is harder."

During a year at Harvard, Ed covered the equivalent of two years of architectural design. He then transferred to M.I.T., because Jacques Carlu was on the staff. Most American architects were building imitations of European styles, but Carlu experimented with unique modern designs.

In 1927 Ed won a scholarship for a two-year period of European travel. In Spain he saw Mies van der Rohe's pavilion at Barcelona. Elsewhere homes, cathedrals, Venetian palaces made him realize that one need only to see the architecture of a civilization to know how people lived, what they believed in, what they felt. Ed walked through and around ancient structures and studied, sketched, and painted them.

Paris excited him. Everywhere he went he saw or heard about men who were doing things in art, music, literature. With students seated at outdoor cafés he entered into conversations in which they redesigned the whole world. While in Stockholm, Sweden, he formed a friendship with Leonard Schultze, senior partner in the New York architectural firm of Schultze and Weaver.

Europe held very little charm for Ed after word came that his brother Hicks had died. His death brought upheaval as well as sorrow. He felt he owed a great deal to Hicks for having interested him in architecture. The open-mindedness and other qualities he had advocated had already taken root.

In September, 1929, Ed landed in New York without a penny. Before the European trip, he had planned to return to Boston, but now he could not bear the sad reminders it would bring of Hicks.

But because of the recent stock market crash, jobs for newcomers in New York were almost nonexistent. Desperate for a lead on any kind of job, Ed called Leonard Schultze, whom he had met in Stockholm. Schultze offered him a position in his firm, then building several hotels. Stone's assignment was interior design for the new Waldorf-Astoria. Schultze's prodigious capacity for work sparked him when his own energies flagged.

During his European travels, Stone, had met and fallen in love with Orlean Vandiver, a distinguished-looking young woman from the South. He had continued to see her. Now, although depression gripped the country, Ed was optimistic about his ability to support a wife. Orlean and he were married in 1931.

After the work available in Schultze's office dried up because of the depression, Stone found employment making models and drawings for the use of architects working on Radio City Music Hall and the Center Theater at Rockefeller Center. Later, he was appointed chief designer. His trellised ceiling for the Starlight Roof and other designs prompted the editorial comment that he was "at the head of the class among young architects."

But after completion of the Rockefeller Center designs, Stone was unemployed. The national depression had worsened, and even seasoned architects were without jobs. He brought an additional handicap upon himself through drinking, which was at times excessive. Stone designed stoves, did advertising layouts, or anything else that came his way. But there were times when he hardly knew where the next meal was coming from for Orlean or himself.

Rose's Restaurant, an unofficial headquarters for architects in New York, became a haven. Rose, a big-hearted Italian woman, gave architects their meals whether they could pay for them or not.

During the lean months, Howard Myers, editor of *Architectural Forum,* acted as guardian angel to young architects by arranging competitions with cash prizes and helping architects get jobs. Myers was especially friendly toward Ed and introduced him to influential persons.

In 1933, industrial designer Richard H. Mandel gave Stone the commission for a large, expensive home at Mt. Kisco, New York. Ed had come back from Europe a devotee of the International style of architecture. He believed that material and functions should dictate the form of a building and that all nonessential trimmings should be eliminated. For the Mandel House he suggested a framework of concrete and steel with continuous strip windows that would permit a panoramic view of the countryside. For the semicircular end of the dining room, he planned to use glass brick, then an innovation.

Ed, Orlean, and baby Edward Junior lived in an old house at the site during the construction period. Whenever blasting was essential, Ed would alert Orlean just before a charge was set off. She would take the baby and run up the hill. The design for the Mandel House had been considered radical, but upon completion it became a showcase for International Style and was widely celebrated.

Stone designed several other International Style houses, but then commissions slowed again. To ease finances he taught night classes at New York University. Their big problem as designers would not be to enclose space but to enclose people, he told his students. Asked if he believed that form follows function, he replied, "Yes, but don't forget that beauty is a function too."

Eager to have an office of his own, Stone set one up in Rockefeller Center, although the depression still gripped the country. A short time later, he and Philip L. Goodwin, a trustee of the Museum of Modern Art in New York, became associated as architects for a new building for the museum. There were many problems during the construction period. A number of persons had to be consulted as to plans, and each had different ideas. To accommodate first one change, then another, Stone made hundreds of drawings and models.

The completed building was a luminous rectangle with a loft that could be rearranged for various kinds of exhibits. Great glass areas provided side lighting for galleries. The ground floor opened on a walled garden. Library, offices, and meeting rooms occupied upper floors, and there was a members' lounge and terrace on the roof.

A. Conger Goodyear, president of the Museum of Modern Art, liked the building so well that he wanted Stone to design a home as a setting for his collection of fine paintings, china, and glassware. On the hilltop site on Long Island, Stone built a house in which the gallery for the art objects formed a kind of spinal column.

Another client, publisher Henry R. Luce, asked for a group of buildings to be placed on a thousand-acre site along the Cooper River in South Carolina. Stone designed a luxurious residence, guest accommodations linked with a walled garden, houses for employees, and a stable group. The house won the Architectural League's gold medal for 1937.

In 1940, Orlean and Ed made a tour of the United States. Of the natural wonders they saw, Stone was perhaps most impressed by the California redwoods. Architecturally he admired the rusticity of Old Faithful Inn in Yellowstone Park and the audacity of Taliesin West in Arizona.

At the Wisconsin Taliesin, Stone visited Frank Lloyd Wright, a long-time architectural and personal hero. Acquaintanceship deepened into friendship. Influenced by Wright and by the buildings he saw on his tour of the country. Stone reconsidered his ideas of architecture. Now it seemed to him that his houses had been too spare and cold.

Soon after Stone's return to New York, he, Howard Myers, and journalist John Fistere were appointed as advisers to the Rockefeller Home Center, a floor in Rockefeller Center's International Building devoted to the display of home furnishings and building products. All three shared in plans for the "House of Ideas," a model house sponsored by *Collier's* magazine to be built on a roof terrace in the Center.

During the planning period, Stone, Fistere, and Myers—all good friends—often met for lunch. Alvar Aalto, Buckminster Fuller, and other distinguished architects sometimes joined them. They approved Stone's idea to use natural redwood for the exterior of the House of Ideas. The completed house, with its floor-to-ceiling sliding windows, received considerable publicity.

By now it had become increasingly evident that America would be involved in World War II raging in Europe. Preparations included new housing for workers who would be flocking to industrial centers. For a defense housing development in Pittsburgh, Stone designed crescent-shaped buildings that fit the sharply sloping terrain.

In 1941, Ed was saddened by the death of his father. His work and the oncoming war helped to steer his thoughts away from the sense of loss. After the sneak attack on Pearl Harbor, Stone enlisted. Because he was thirty-nine, he was not accepted for active duty but served as chief of the U.S. Army's Planning and Design Section.

With the help of a corps of assistants, Stone designed a number of airports and installations but had very little opportunity to carry out original ideas. He did, however, become acquainted with the organizational problems of large-scale planning.

At the end of the war, Orlean and Ed leased a house at Great Neck, on Long Island, and he had his office there. Later he moved his office to New York, where his young nephew Karl J. Holzinger joined him and became a valuable colleague.

Stone's postwar houses ranged from a luxurious one for W. T. Grant at Greenwich, Connecticut, to simple ones that could be built by the owner. The *Ladies' Home Journal* publicized one in which precut columns and roof rafters on a standard unit of measurement made construction easier for amateurs.

In his efforts to produce homes that would best meet the needs of their occupants. Stone explored the living habits of his clients.

What will make the place they live in more beautiful? he would ask himself. What will make their lives easier, more comfortable?

He regarded any house as the joint product of client and architect. Once, on a watercolor that reproduced the client's home, he wrote, "Architects, Mr. and Mrs. John Doe. Edward D. Stone, Associate."

He liked to provide quality and yet never wanted to overcharge a client. At times his commissions allowed for almost no profit. An accountant who went over his books at one time told him, "Mr. Stone, you are living without any visible means of support."

Classes he taught at Yale University helped eke out his income. With students he took a strong stand against what he called architectural illiteracy. Would-be architects, he said, should read history and travel.

"You cannot understand a building from studying pictures of it," he insisted. "You have to walk through and around it, conjure up the time in which it was built, know the source of its inspiration."

During the late 1940's, Stone redesigned the old Victoria Theater on Broadway and converted it from legitimate theater to a first-run movie house. For the interior he achieved an unusual effect by hanging the walls with a metal fabric made of stampings from discarded movie reels.

The biggest project Stone had undertaken up to that time was El Panama Hotel, financed by the Panamanian government, private subscription, and the Export-Import Bank. On a hilltop two miles out of Panama City, only part of the hotel, had air conditioning. Rooms that had no artificial temperature control were placed one deep along an open gallery and equipped with jalousies that gave cross ventilation. Public rooms on the main floor were separated only by screens and opened on both sides to terrraces and gardens. There was a roof-top restaurant and an outdoor dancing area. El Panama set the style for resort hotels from Hawaii to Istanbul.

When Stone designed the Bay Roc Hotel in Montego Bay, Jamaica, he placed the public rooms in one building and the bedrooms in another, so guests not interested in revelry could have quiet. Both structures fronted on gardens with luxuriant foliage.

Architectural success was marred by what was happening in Stone's personal life. When Howard Myers died, Stone felt he had lost an incomparable friend. At home, his marriage was going on the rocks.

Stone was very fond of Orlean and his two sons, but his work left very little time to do things with the family. Normally the hours spent at the drafting board seemed short because he loved his work, but Orlean felt neglected. Ed tried to give more of himself to shared projects after she accused him of being married to his architecture, but he was often absent-minded and dreamy. Orlean finally left, taking the boys with her. Even after the divorce they remained friends, but for Ed his home had become only a place of loneliness.

The pressure of commissions forced Stone to keep his mind on his work. For the University of Arkansas, he designed a Medical Center and a Fine Arts Center that housed facilities for the teaching of architecture, painting, sculpture, music, and drama. An exhibition gallery linked a classroom building with one housing the concert hall, theater, and library. In recognition of Stone's contributions, the university awarded him an honorary degree. The Medical Center won an honor award from the American Institute of Architects.

Houses still claimed a share of Stone's attention. One of his favorites was designed for Dr. J. Allen Robinson at Harrison, Arkansas. It was built of logs because Stone felt they fit best with the Ozark mountain setting. The main house, guest houses, and garage area were linked by a loggia—a roofed open gallery.

In 1953, Stone was invited to Paris as consultant on the design for a hospital. On the flight there he sat next to a young brunette whose beauty and charm made him very conscious of his rumpled tweeds. She identified herself as Maria Elena Torch. Fashion Editor of *Fashion and Travel,* she was bound for Rome but planned a stopover in Paris.

During their conversation, Maria revealed that she was of Spanish and Italian parentage. Originally from Cleveland, she now lived in New York. Her father was an architect, and she had always been interested in the arts. Stone was fascinated by her fire and vivacity. In Paris he bombarded her with flowers and theater tickets. Before Maria left for Rome, she and Ed were engaged.

Eleven months later, Maria was again in Rome and Ed was in India, inspecting the site for the American Embassy at New Delhi. They agreed that they would meet and wed in Beirut, Lebanon, where Stone was building the luxurious Phoenicia Intercontinental Hotel. They were married in the palace of an archbishop of the Greek Orthodox Church, although neither was a member of this faith.

From Beirut the Stones continued around the world to New York. Maria's belief in his genius gave Ed impetus in his work and altered old habits. He stopped drinking. His appearance was still at times disheveled, but having Maria lay out appropriate clothes made it easier to keep spruced up. Because he was incurably absent-minded, Maria drove the car, and made him put on shoes when she caught him leaving for the office in red house slippers, but she never bossed him on things that mattered.

With better organization of his daily life, Stone could achieve more than before. He continued work on the Embassy and other projects; he lectured at Yale, Princeton, New York University, Cornell, and the University of Arkansas. The architect, Stone told students, must be first of all a creative artist. He could depend on contractors and engineers to carry out the mechanics, but he must create the design for the building. Stone captured the imagination of architectural students by telling them that they must do more than take into account culture, climate, site, and purpose of structure. Buildings must also have drama.

When he talked informally with boys not yet in college, Stone always encouraged those who had any inclinations toward becoming architects. In his eyes there was no more rewarding profession. As preparation, he advised them to draw, make models, make plans of their own homes. "Learn to recognize situations that are beautiful," he told them.

When Stone had a breather between lectures, Maria and he bought an old brownstone house in New York City. The first thing Ed did was to strip the face of the building and put glass all the way to the top. About twelve inches in front of the glass, he placed a lacy grille or lattice of terra-cotta that made it possible to see out but not be seen.

In their drawing room he left the dark wood paneling and the exuberantly carved fireplace but paved the floor with white marble to relate it to the dining area and the porch. Furnishings throughout the spacious home were lavish—marble tables, Spanish Renaissance chairs, Venetian velvet hangings. There were hundreds of books, paintings, sculpture, and Shoji screens. Porch furniture was of the type originally designed in collaboration with Senator Fulbright, a friend since boyhood.

Fulbright had wanted more marketable products than the plows and wagons his farm implement company had been turning out. Stone had suggested outdoor furniture, using plow handles for chair legs. Ozark basket weavers provided hickory backs and chair seats. This sturdy furniture, thought Stone, would meet the needs of their baby son Benjamin Hicks when he was old enought to use it.

A short time after the remodeling was completed, Frank Lloyd Wright, "Uncle Frank" to little Hicks, came to visit. "I'm an old crank who never has anything nice to say," Wright told Ed, "but I'm raving."

□ 172

Graf House, Dallas, Texas, by Edward Durell Stone. 1956. Photograph by Lisanti, courtesy the architect.

Both Wright and Maria encouraged Stone to go further in his revolt against the steel, the slablike surface, and the glass façades of the International Style. In a house designed for Mr. and Mrs. Bruno Graf in Dallas, Texas, he tried to bring back some of the elegance and individuality that had preceded the machine age. All the rooms of the masonry buildings were paved with white marble and opened on courtyards. Arabesque screens separated specialized living areas. Dining room furniture was placed on a circular marble island in a rectangular pool. Diners reached the area by crossing a bridge.

During the 1950's, Stone had to travel a great deal to lecture, teach, and supervise projects.

"When I'm not at my drafting board, I'm on a jet," he told Maria. But he enjoyed travel when Maria went with him, and she often did.

Stone spent six months in Lima, Peru, where he collaborated on plans for the impressive Social Security Hospital. On side trips into the countryside, he collected fine samples of pre-Inca pottery.

One of the things Stone appreciated about commissions that took him to many parts of the world was the opportunity it gave him to study old buildings. History, he felt, had been written in buildings as well as in books. He was always on the alert for ideas that would help him be a better architect.

In Instanbul he marveled at the Byzantine-style church of Santa Sophia. It was proof, he thought, that masterpieces of architecture may endure and exert an influence for thousands of years. In Greece he concluded that their architecture had never been surpassed for its harmony, beauty, and refined proportions.

Once, after he viewed the Parthenon, he said to Maria, "If the Greeks took three hundred years to come up with the Parthenon, we should be more patient."

Of all the cities the Stones visited, Ed liked Venice best. There, visitors had to park their cars in garages outside the heart of the city. This eliminated traffic snarls, fumes, and honking. Venice, Ed told Maria, could be paralleled in the United States by having downtown shopping areas reserved for pedestrians.

Stone could never consider only the scene of the project of the moment. It took months or even years to complete a building, and in the meantime he always had others under way in scattered locations. Architects, he thought, should be ambassadors of good will; and when he built in foreign lands, he did his best to maintain a friendly relationship with local builders and craftsmen.

For the United States Embassy at New Delhi, workmen brought their families and lived on the grounds in straw-matting houses. They fashioned concrete and marble and then finished and polished these materials by hand.

Before the Embassy was completed, Stone was planning the U.S. Pavilion for the Brussels World Fair scheduled for 1958. The State Department had asked the American Institute of Architects to select a designer, and a committee of five had chosen Stone.

After a visit to the site, he sketched a circular structure to be built of transparent plastic and gold-colored steel. But the enormous free-span circular roof that he wanted presented unusual problems. Engineering consultants finally suggested a roof that would use the principle of a bicycle wheel, with an outer ring of concrete connected by radiating spokes of steel cables to an inner ring. Both rings would be supported by thin steel columns.

The outer covering of translucent plastic panels was fabricated in the United States and air-lifted to Brussels. An auditorium half underground snuggled in the shoulder of a hill adjacent to the pavilion. Inside the pavilion there was a circular lagoon surrounded by eleven great willow trees that had been growing on the site for years.

A mesh made from gilded aluminum discs created a gold curtain over the entire interior. Exhibits showing phases of American life and cultural achievements were to be exhibited on islands in the lagoon and on mezzanines in the building.

175 □

One day when the pavilion was almost finished, Stone, his Homburg awry, drove up in front of the building. The white transparent panels made it look light and airy. The gilded columns and gold-colored escutcheons glistened in the bright sunshine. Stone could imagine the color and holiday atmosphere that would be added by placement of the flags of the states of the United States.

"Wow!" he exclaimed, as he grinned with delight.

The public responded with equal fervor. "Spectacular ... a fine showcase for the United States," editors commented. The New York *Herald Tribune* called it "one of the most attractive structures in international exhibition history."

Stone had become a contender for world architectural honors.

After completion of the Brussels Pavilion, the Stones took a vacation at a villa near Venice. From there they traveled to Russia in response to official invitations. His political views clashed with those of his hosts, but harmonious discussions with his colleagues proved his contention that architecture is a universal language. Two things he liked very much about Russia—the absence of out-door advertising and of traffic jams.

From Russia, the Stones went to New Delhi for dedication of the American Embassy. The two-story structure stood on a podium or platform. Aluminum columns covered with gold leaf supported the portico and gave opulence. Arabesque grilles of white marble and gold surrounded the building and made it shimmer like an expensive present. A canopy separated from the second floor ceiling by several feet shaded the building and created a heat-dissipating breezeway.

Offices were placed around a cooling water garden with plant-ing pools and jets of water roofed over by aluminum mesh. Some who worked in the Embassy thought it more of an esthetic than a practical success—for one thing, the grills absorbed enough heat during the day to counteract night cooling.

United States Pavilion, Brussels, Belgium, by Edward Durell Stone. 1957. Photograph courtesy the architect.

But the Embassy became one of the most talked about buildings in the world. Frank Lloyd Wright teasingly told Ed that because he owed much of his inspiration to his wife he ought to call the structure the Taj Maria. Then he went on to say that this was one of the finest buildings in the last hundred years. Architect Philip Johnson's comment was, "The New Delhi Embassy? How could I help loving it? It's a jewel."

Despite globe-girdling undertakings, Stone still did a great deal of building in the United States and also became involved in city planning, about which he had very definite views. Every city, he thought, should have an agency that cherished beauty and enforced not merely a building code but a minimum esthetic standard. Buildings, like people, should be protected from shoddy surroundings. In new housing areas, provisions ought always to be made for parks.

Civic buildings should be planned to harmonize with one another. "I have little love for glass," Stone explained, "but if I were requested to design a building in an area where that material is dominant I should feel obligated to do the best I could with glass, to preserve the flavor of the neighborhood."

Stone did not want automobiles and pedestrians mixed. He favored closed malls for shopping areas. "Main Street," he said, "should be a pedestrian oasis."

Stone had the opportunity to carry out some of his ideas when he designed civic centers for Akron, New Orleans, and Tulsa.

Campuses took more of Stone's time than civic centers. He planned buildings for Mohawk Valley Technical Institute, Vanderbilt University, the California Institute of Technology, Harvey Mudd College, and others. For the University of South Carolina he designed a white marble library and a dormitory. At the University of Chicago he built the Center for Continuing Education, combining hotel facilities with conference rooms.

Stone did not believe that students should bring automobiles to college. A campus, he continued, should be for meditation and study—cars tempted students away from their books. When he planned a college campus for the State University of New York at Albany, he discouraged motorists by the omission of roadways. Cars had to be parked around the periphery. But he spared students from walking great distances by grouping all academic facilities in the center of the grounds. Students lived in towering twenty-story dormitories placed at the four corners of the campus.

Campus planning took Stone abroad again when he designed the U.S.-sponsored International College at Beirut. He arranged circular reinforced concrete buildings in an ellipse on the hillside site. Central rotundas gave access to classrooms. At intervals on the campus he placed lagoons, terraces, arcades, and covered walkways.

Between campuses, city plans, and embassies, Stone squeezed plans for hospitals, medical, and pharmaceutical buildings. Before he started a sketch for any of these, he gave close attention to the patterns of daily life of those who would use the building. He conferred with physicians, pharmacists, nurses, technicians, and custodians who would be involved.

For the Stanford University Medical Center at Palo Alto, Stone built a three-story building with all rooms related to landscape gardens. At Carmel, California, he designed the Community Hospital with no institutional corridors. Each cluster of four rooms had access to a covered porch.

When Arthur Hanisch was discussing plans for the Stuart Company's pharmaceutical plant in Pasadena he told Stone, "I'll give you a free hand and won't even look until the plant is finished."

Stone had a three-acre site and three million dollars to work with on a plant for one hundred and forty employees. He designed a white building with a gold façade and gold-lacquered columns. In accordance with his belief that bodies of water enhance a building and lend a sense of repose, Stone used black-bottomed reflecting pools that extended under the cantilevered grille walls and gave the building a hovering effect. A dining area in one of the inner patios

179 □

had mother-of-pearl light globes suspended in big saucers of vegetation.

Hanisch had kept hands off as promised. On opening day, as he made the rounds with Stone, he kept exclaiming, "Beautiful!" At one point he stopped and, with tears in his eyes, said, "Ed, it's fantastic, it's—it's out of this world!"

The Pasadena "pill factory" won highly favorable comment. It was in International Style, said one reporter, but it had been gift wrapped.

Other public buildings at about this time included a hotel in Karachi, Pakistan, the Chatham Motor Hotel in Pittsburgh, and the Reef Point Hotel in Laguna Beach, California. The Reef Point Hotel had a sawtooth plan that gave every room an ocean view.

On some of his projects, Stone had cooperation from Edward, Jr., who had become a landscape architect and had an office in Fort Lauderdale, Florida. Ed thought his son had a great deal of talent and enjoyed having him work at his side.

Although Stone had designed an impressive number of public buildings, he had not turned his back on domestic architecture. A house, he thought, should offer comfort and convenience, but it should also exalt the spirit. A beautiful home could contribute to the manners, dignity, and graciousness of the family who lived in it.

Because houses on individual lots dissipate miles of land and cause urban sprawl, Stone became very interested in wall-to-wall housing. But ways had to be found to insure row-house dwellers beauty, privacy, and quietude. In Pompeii he had seen atrium houses—square houses built around a square garden. Why couldn't these solve the problem of row-house dwellers? Stone wondered.

A spur to exploration came when the editors of *Life* magazine asked Stone to design a housing plan for their readers. The row-house development that he drew up set aside a sizable plot for a public park. Neat, compact groups of houses clustered around U-shaped courts that served as recreational areas. Each house had a glass wall that opened on an enclosed patio.

The interiors had two-story living rooms with balcony bedrooms insulated by heavy sound-insulating curtains. They gave the impression of space, warmth, graciousness, even of grandeur.

Stone's houses and public buildings won numerous awards. He was named a member of the United States National Institute of Arts and Letters. He received a medal of honor from the New York chapter of the American Institute of Architects and the grand prize from the Pittsburgh Glass Competition. Several times he won the New York Architectural League Medal for Domestic Architecture. A number of magazines carried feature articles by or about him. *Vogue* magazine referred to Stone as an architect who dazzled his colleagues and the public.

To handle the commissions that poured in, Stone set up offices in New York, Fayetteville, and Palo Alto. His Sixty-fifth Street office was staffed by a manager, three secretaries, and around twenty young architects, some of them former students. It was gratifying to Stone to be surrounded by dedicated young men. He liked to think that he was producing architects as well as architecture.

"We've neglected our obligation to plan well for future generations," he told his assistants. He urged them to correct unfortunate environments. If even a handful of dedicated architects worked toward this goal, there could be one of those soaring periods in history when beautiful buildings could be put up that would be inherited by generations to come.

Stone transmitted his leanings toward certain architectural materials and features. He preferred marble to wood, and he had a special fondness for grilles because they give privacy and lend patterns and color to what would otherwise be bare façades. Grilles also shelter large areas of glass, that are hard to heat in winter and cool in summer, and thus reduce air-conditioning loads.

181 □

"Not all architects share my enthusiasm for grilles," said Stone one day, and grinned, remembering Finnish-born Eero Saarinen's comment that Stone's friends ought to wrestle his grilles away from him. Some architects had nicknamed him Mr. Peekaboo, because of his liking for the half concealed, half revealed.

Although Stone revealed his preferences, he wanted no imitation of his own or anyone else's buildings. "Do be guided, however, by ageless patterns," he warned young architects. "And do not in your quest for originality create trivialities." Style, he told them, was less important than attitudes. "The architect must first be a humanitarian."

During the early 1960's, Stone's building activities went on at a furious pace. He designed an Institute of Nuclear Sciences and Engineering for Pakistan's new capital at Islamabad, Beckman Auditorium for the California Institute of Technology, and main and branch libraries for Palo Alto.

The North Carolina legislative Building at Raleigh, North Carolina, with an exterior of white marble, had underground parking and service facilities. Oxidized green copper covered the pyramids of the roof.

Other projects in the East included Sherwood Apartments at Asheville, North Carolina, Carlton House luxury apartments in Philadelphia, and the West Side Apartments that were part of an urban renewal project in New York City.

Stone had always liked to design churches, because such buildings are motivated by considerations of the spirit and are likely to survive for generations. He had already built Methodist and Presbyterian churches and a synagogue. The small All Souls Unitarian Church in Schenectady, New York, was built with seats in a semicircle around the altar, giving the minister a close relationship with the congregation. Now he designed an abbey for Trappist monks on Luce-donated land near Charleston, South Carolina. So the monks of this order committed to silence could build their own abbey, Stone planned do-it-yourself concrete and brick.

As commissions for churches, libraries, houses, plants, and office buildings poured in, Maria, who was businesslike and intelligent, shared Ed's work. But she could be outspoken and tempestuous if he ignored family life for too long. Then Ed would follow the advice he sometimes gave to others, "Take time out to sit among the flowers in your garden, or look into the eyes of the woman you love." He would also romp with his son Hicks. Maria's gaiety and humor would soon reappear.

But recesses were brief. Some new project was always luring Stone to the drafting board. His first real skyscraper was designed for Childs Security Corporation. To cut down glare he avoided an all-glass façade and used vision panels instead. For the multistory Perpetual Savings and Loan Association Building in Los Angeles, Stone devised tiers of concrete parabolic arches with glass set three feet behind them. At the level of each floor on the outside of the building, he placed planting beds. The exterior became a series of hanging gardens with tropical vegetation.

Factories that looked like a chunk of masonry set down in a parking lot had long troubled Stone. He contended that buildings of good design combined with plazas or a grassy site in open country were soul-satisfying and were also good business. He was delighted when Yardley of London, Inc., at Totowa, New Jersey, gave him room to spread out. He surrounded the steel and white-brick-veneer building with pools and plantings and gave it a country-club atmosphere.

Among other buildings during this period were a sales office for Pakistan International Airways at Rawalpindi, a building for the Water and Power Development Authority at Lahore in West Pakistan, a mosque for the Pakistan International Airways at Karachi, and luxury apartments landscaped by his son Edward, Jr., at Palm Beach, Florida.

183 □

As he traveled from Palm Beach to Pakistan or from New Jersey to California, Stone was often interviewed or asked to appear on radio and television shows. Interviewers described him as a big, informal, handsome man who was soft of speech and had a habitual expression of kindness.

His speech became less soft whenever he was questioned on the subject of billboards, neon signs, or automobiles, which he detested. He called billboards "eye-searing blasts of commercialism." At one interview he asserted, "The automobile, the neon sign, the atomic pile—all are lethal unless controlled." When the staff of *U.S. News and World Report* interviewed Stone, he said, "We have made a choice between people and the automobile, with the automobile clearly the winner."

Automobiles were forgotten when Stone set to work designing the Gallery of Modern Art, on Columbus Circle in New York, for Huntington Hartford, who had put up seven and a half million dollars to incorporate his own private collection of paintings as a permanent exhibit. Museums were nothing new to Stone. He had designed the Commercial Museum in Philadelphia; the Ponce Museum of Art at Ponce, Puerto Rico, and the Carmelita Cultural Center in Pasadena, California, that included a museum, concert hall, and art gallery.

When it was completed, the Gallery of Modern Art presented a smooth white marble-and-concrete surface, interrupted only by graceful arches at street level and two upper floors. One editor commented that it successfully combined the stately beauty of a Manhattan Taj Mahal with the functionality of an automation punch card. The punch-card effect came from rows of small circular holes that lined the structure's corners and were as unusual as they were effective.

Stone had another opportunity to provide a showcase for culture when he was asked to design the opera house, concert hall, and theater for the National Cultural Center—the John F. Kennedy

The Gallery of Modern Art, New York City, by Edward Durell Stone. Photograph by Arnold Eagle.

Center for the Performing Arts. He could not at first come up with a plan that would make the Center harmonize with existing buildings and yet be modern in spirit. Any building, he thought, should express the architect's views about life and art. It must be as personal as his own handwriting.

He drew several plans, but the one he favored called for three auditoriums arranged in a row but separated by entrance lobbies. Foyers would overlook the Potomac River. The roofed area would be devoted to restaurants with an area between them that could be used for outdoor balls, band concerts, and art exhibits.

In 1964 Stone's name came to the fore when the Building Stone Institute named him Architect of the Year and the National Geographic Society dedicated the headquarters he had designed for them in Washington, D.C. The structure rose from a marble podium with a sheltered promenade and soared upward to a slotted canopy that Stone called its hat. Vertical fins of white marble added beauty but also shielded occupants of the building from too much sun. Insets of black Swedish granite gave a decorative trim.

So the building would reflect loveliness at night, Stone arranged for lights to shine from the upper terrace along the sides of each fin. Underground spotlights lit up magnolia trees and shrubs. The colonnaded first floor was devoted to Explorer's Hall, with exhibits portraying man's exploration of jungles, peaks, polar regions, and the world beneath the sea. In the cafeteria on the tenth floor, done in Italian red glass tile, the employees could look out over the city while they ate.

The building added to Stone's fame, but his name became even more widely known through his contributions to the World's Fair in 1964. The Central American States Pavilion had a loggia surrounding open-air marketplaces. A sheltered tropical garden flanked a hall for concerts and folk dancing.

Stone had also designed the Christian Science Pavilion that provided a reading area and exhibits. Visitors entered through a circular element open to the sky. Inside, a glazed roof provided light for interior planting.

For the House of Good Taste exhibit, he built a square-roofed home with latticed overhang. Core of the house was a spacious, glass-dome atrium with a circular reflecting pool. Doors and windows of all corner rooms opened onto walled courtyards.

Between designs, through articles, interviews, and speeches, Stone carried on a relentless campaign for beauty in our buildings and in our nation.

In a talk given at the Universalist Church in New York City, he said, "In fifty years—we do everything rapidly—we've converted this country from one of the most beautiful to one of the ugliest."

Over and over again, in different words but expressing the same ideas, Stone emphasized the "colossal mess we've made of the face of our country." Bulldozers, he said were "assassinating the country-side with ugliness."

In cities he saw "neon jungles" and buildings that revealed their designers as "catchpenny materialists with a blatant screeching insistence on commercialism. If you haven't got beauty, you haven't got architecture," he told one reporter.

Beautiful buildings, he thought, encouraged persons to strive for higher qualities. It depressed him that city officials often seemed able to afford everything except beauty.

Permanence as well as beauty became almost an obsession with Stone. On the WCBS radio show *Horizons,* he said, "It's all wrong, the temporary quality of our buildings, you know? They're built for early obsolescence. . . . Everything's substandard." Elsewhere he said, "Architecture is not like millinery. Fashions pass, but buildings must remain."

Stone's use of marble and rugged materials, his sense of proportion, and his classic elegance made his own buildings both beautiful and permanent. His revolt against modern functionalism, which he said gave a scorched-earth appearance, resulted in lush, magnificent buildings. His structures, ranging from homes and hospitals to atomic plants and factories, and the way he combined the austere and the highly decorative, earned him a reputation as one of the most versatile designers of the century. His buildings, both in their number and quality, have made major contributions to changing the shape of our world.

His life has had some of the qualities of his architecture. "Ed's architecture is honest," Frank Lloyd Wright said of him. "And so is he."

As friendly as he is honest, he has won the respect of monks, millionaires, housewives, and hospital board members. Beneath his uninhibited manner and informal speech is a seriousness and dedication to the best in architecture and in life. He is also enthusiastic. "I love my work," he tells interviewers. "To me it is the greatest kind of play."

On more than one occasion he has said, "Let's strike the bell for beauty." Edward D. Stone has been very busy striking that bell.

EIGHT

EERO SAARINEN

Second-Generation Genius

It would have been surprising if Eero Saarinen had not become an architect. As a child he almost lived under his father's drafting table in the large studio living room of the Saarinen home in Kirkunummi, Finland. Eliel had won many awards for his buildings and had been town planner for Helsinki, Finland, and Canberra, Australia. He had also designed the thirty-eight-room home in which the family lived. His wife Louise, or Loja, was a gifted sculptor and textile designer and frequently helped Eliel with his plans. Eero's older sister Eve-Lisa, nicknamed Pipsan, was a talented artist.

Eero loved being included in the creative projects always under way in the family studio. His father, who called him "Poju" or Sonny, encouraged him to paint, model, and make designs out of matchsticks.

Although sensitive and serious, Eero was robustly energetic and liked to ski and explore the woods surrounding the house. He also

189 □

enjoyed the high talk and folk singing when musicians, sculptors, actors, and architects came to visit. Among them was the Finnish composer Jean Sibelius.

While still very young, Eero took lessons from the Hungarian sculptor Maróti, a friend of the family. Maróti made him draw from nature, study anatomy, and do things over and over. Eero's father was exacting, too, and held him to the rule that if he started a project he must finish it, even if he lost interest. One day Eero was working on a matchbox emblem to enter in a contest. When only half finished, he went off to play with another child. His father met him at the door when he came home. "Competition," he said kindly but firmly, "comes first. Girls second."

Eliel also demanded excellence. "But," he said, "remember that there is no final excellence without a love of one's work."

When Eero was twelve, he entered a contest sponsored by a Swedish newspaper in which contestants were required to write a story and illustrate it with pictures made of matches. Eero, with a few suggestions from his mother, contrived a wild tale of a young woman whose suitors, jealous of one another, finally burned themselves up. He was elated when he captured first prize and received a cash award. The whole family celebrated the victory.

Later in the week, the Saarinens had another pleasant surprise when word came that Eliel's design for a structure to house the Chicago *Tribune* had won second place in an international competition. The award amounted to twenty thousand dollars.

Eliel decided to dip into the prize money for a trip to the United States, where he could meet colleagues and study architectural styles. The letters he wrote back to the family expressed surprise that he was so well known in the United States. Several universities offered him a position. He liked this land and wanted his family to join him. In April, 1923, Eero, Pipsan, and their mother met Eliel in New York.

The following autumn they went to Ann Arbor, where Eliel

Eero Saarinen

had been invited to teach architecture at the University of Michigan. When the opportunity came for Eliel to design the Cranbrook Academy, the family moved to Bloomfield Hills, Michigan. Cranbrook, an arts and crafts school for boys, was financed by a Detroit millionaire, George G. Booth.

Eero attended Baldwin High School in Birmingham, only a few miles away. He had always liked to read, but now he became interested in the biographies of important persons. In out-of-school hours he often drafted alongside his father and absorbed his philosophy that work, to be convincing, must be honest, a true expression of one's thoughts and emotions.

After Eliel accepted the post as Director of Cranbrook Academy, Eero found many ways to use his architectural skills. The whole family shared in finishing Kingswood, a school for girls authorized by Cranbrook administrators as part of an expansion program. Loja wove rugs, draperies, and furniture coverings fine in craftsmanship

191 ☐

and original in design. Pipsan handled interior decoration for the auditorium and the dining room, and Eero designed the furniture.

The family again cooperated in furnishing the home Eliel planned for them. Almost every item was made by some member of the family or by friends who were artists. A wing at the back provided a studio and classroom for apprentices and students in the department of postgraduate architecture and city planning founded by Eliel.

Each summer the Saarinens returned to Finland to visit their old home and to renew friendships. On one trip Eliel persuaded their good friend Carl Milles to join them as a resident sculptor at Cranbrook Academy. Milles praised the sculptural quality of Eero's furniture and fanned his interest in sculpture. Eero carved a figure that won first prize in a national soap sculpture contest.

By the time he graduated from high school in 1929, Eero was not sure whether he wanted to be an architect or a sculptor. After a year at the Académie de la Grande Chaumière in Paris, he returned to his first love. In 1931 he entered the Yale School of Architecture.

Shyness bothered Eero, but he won friends through his lack of affectation, dry wit, and dead-pan humor. The Yale School of Architecture had its students enter Beaux-Arts competitions. Resourceful, brilliant, and already skilled in designing, Eero once received eight medals in a row, but all for second place. Fellow students teasingly called him Second Medal Saarinen. Yale awarded him a medal for winning a record number of awards, and he placed third in a contest for a design for a post office for Helsinki, Finland.

After he had earned his Bachelor of Arts degree, Eero went abroad on a Charles O. Matcham fellowship which would pay expenses for a year of travel in Europe. He ate, slept, and dreamed architecture and studied buildings from the Piazza San Marco in Italy to cathedrals in France.

Travel in Europe, Palestine, and Egypt made Eero aware that

architecture includes man's total surroundings, from chairs to cities. An invitation to collaborate with Finnish architect Jarl Eklund in rebuilding the Swedish Playhouse in Helsinki gave him another year overseas.

Eager to become a practicing architect, Eero returned to America in July, 1936. He took a job with the Flint Institute of Planning but soon returned to Cranbrook to assist his father and to teach design at the Academy. Eero was determined not to become a blind imitator. But he admired his father's architecture and humbly accepted principles he set forth. One of these was to design a thing by considering its next largest context—a chair in a room, a room in a house, a house in a neighborhood, a neighborhood in a city.

Eero and his father worked together on the Kleinhaus Music Hall in Buffalo, New York. In shape the building resembled a violin. Inside, there were two halls, the larger one seating about three thousand persons. The building won high praise from both musicians and the public.

Duties at the Academy took much of Eero's time. Among the students at Cranbrook was a New York sculptress, Lillian Swann, who had come to study ceramics. The vivid brunette and Eero were drawn together by similar tastes in art and sports. Eero had always liked to ski, and Lily had been a member of the American Women's Olympic Ski Team. Friendship led to marriage.

In 1939, Eero, his father, and Robert F. Swanson, an architect and interior designer who had married Pipsan, formed the firm of Saarinen, Swanson, and Saarinen. The three were in agreement that they would never take on so many projects that quality would be sacrificed.

Eero worked with his father on a number of challenging commissions. Two jointly designed plans were the First Christian Church at Columbus, Indiana, and the Crow Island School at Winnetka, Illinois. The school was an astonishing building for its time. L-shaped classrooms with an abundance of light and air opened on small courts with shrubs and flagstone walks. Each classroom had a work area with a sink. Eero designed furniture scaled to the needs of children, and his wife Lily did ceramic sculptures that were incorporated into the outer wall of the building.

After the Crow Island School was built, the Saarinens concentrated on a design for the Smithsonian Art Gallery to be entered in a competition. The Saarinens won, but Congress failed to provide funds for construction.

Eero's disappointment was offset somewhat by the success of his furniture. For a competition sponsored by the Museum of Modern Art, he collaborated with his good friend Charles Eames. Charles, who had come to Cranbrook as a young man to work with Eliel, had a great deal of talent. The models of body-molded living room chairs and sectional living-room furniture that the two young men submitted won two first prizes. Eero and Charles were delighted when their chairs were caricatured by Al Capp in "Li'l Abner."

The outbreak of World War II keenly affected the Saarinens. Friendships had been kept alive by yearly visits to Finland, and now these friends and relatives were involved in a life-and-death struggle. But Eero's first loyalty was to his adopted country, and in 1940 he became a naturalized citizen.

Wartime slow-down in civilian construction affected the firm, but Eero and his father went ahead with plans for the Opera Shed at the Berkshire Music Center in Lennox, Massachusetts. Eero's hand was clearly visible in the strict, functional design. Acoustics and lighting were so good that the official of a broadcasting company said, "One can credit the designers with having achieved next to the impossible."

The firm also designed the Tabernacle Church of Christ in Columbus, Indiana. Members of the congregation felt it had a profound effect on churchgoers and on the community.

As a contribution to the defense effort, Eero helped his father with war housing projects at Willow Run and Center Line, Michigan, and served in the Office of Strategic Services in Washington, D.C.

Eero's interest in housing spurred him to enter a contest sponsored by *Arts and Architecture* magazine. Interior designer Oliver Lindquist worked with him. Their plan for two prefabricated units that could be assembled in any combination won first place.

During the final stage of the war, Lily and Eero bought an old brick farmhouse built around 1860 and located outside Bloomfield Hills. Eero would have liked to design his own home, but Lily and he decided it would be a challenge to remodel this one to meet their needs and those of their children, Eric and Susan.

They played up old Victorian features, but Eero planned to design modern furniture as soon as he had time. Meanwhile they improvised temporary furnishings. Eliel made them a dining room table with a marble pedestal. Art objects abounded throughout the house. Of Lily's highly original sculptured works, Eero especially admired a three-toed sloth and the caricature of a friend.

In the postwar years, the Saarinen firm became one of the best known in the country. Eero, now thirty-seven, was finding it hard to work in the shadow of his father's fame. At times he had an insatiable desire to prove himself. Yet he wanted to have a partnership with his father, whose wit, imagination, and wisdom he so much admired.

Eero had a good opportunity to experiment with his own ideas when he heard of a competition for a design for a park and memorial in St. Louis, Missouri, to honor former president Thomas Jefferson and the nation's march westward. A committee of citizens sponsoring the Jefferson National Expansion Memorial would guarantee a cash prize amounting to forty thousand dollars. Congress would appropriate funds for construction.

After Eero had seen the site bordering the Mississippi River, he thought it called for an upward thrusting form that would catch the spirit of a city proud of its past as the gateway to the West. A gigantic arch of shining steel kept coming to mind, but he wasn't sure engineers could build the memorial he envisioned. Eero almost never achieved a design in a great flash of inspiration. On this plan he worked slowly and discussed his ideas with Lily and with associates in the firm.

He finally designed a 630-foot arch of stainless steel that tapered to the apex. On the levee side there would be a monumental stairway. An observation bubble reached by steps and by an elevator in the hollow core of the legs of the arch would give sightseers a view of the heartland of America. In the eighty-acre park surrounding the memorial, pools, rock outcroppings, trees, and paths would repeat the curve of the arch. There would be an underground museum with two theaters, a tea terrace, and a frontier village.

The judges were unanimous in awarding Eero the prize. Publication of the design brought diverse reactions. Critics said the arch looked like a giant croquet wicket or a stupendous hairpin. But Aline B. Louchheim, Associate Art Editor for the New York *Times* and author of *5,000 Years of Art,* said it had a simplicity that would guarantee its timeliness. Others called it "a thing of clean beauty on a grand scale . . . an act of mind and heart."

Construction was delayed because Congress procrastinated in appropriating funds. Meanwhile, Eero, never completely satisfied with his products, built and rebuilt models of the arch and refined the structural steel frame.

As commissions for other projects poured into the office, he often felt under pressure. Skiing with Lily and his two children helped him relax. But even on skis, Eero would have his mind on current projects, many of them for schools or campuses.

Before starting on a women's dormitory for Antioch College at Yellow Springs, Ohio, he studied the whole village until he could have reproduced it from memory. He acquainted himself with future plans of the college and the village.

Industrial commissions also came into the office. Shortly after the name of the firm was changed to Saarinen, Saarinen, and Associates, they captured the most important industrial assignment in postwar United States, the Technical Center for General Motors. The company was prepared to spend a hundred million dollars on buildings and a 350-acre site outside Detroit.

To Eliel, the project, which would take years to construct, looked staggering, and he turned much of the responsibility over to Eero. As always when approaching an architectural problem, Eero asked himself, what is its essence? What methods, what materials will capture that essence?

For General Motors, Eero wanted to symbolize the dramatic relationships among men, science, and industry. As for methods and materials, steel and precision seemed essential. Each of five staff organizations—Research, Process Development, Engineering, Styling, and the Service Center—would have its own complex of buildings.

Eero agreed with his father that the separate units could be unified through use of a green belt, pools, fountains, and a twenty-acre lake. When Eliel suggested contrasts in height, Eero thought vertical accent could be achieved through use of a stainless steel water tower.

The interior would, for the most part, be column free, and office paneling would be interchangeable. Eero suggested luminous ceilings for the drafting rooms and injection of color into machines and mechanical facilities. He studied and revised designs and built mock-ups to be tested under outdoor conditions.

The Saarinens, with help from associates and engineers, developed some ingenious structural devices for the General Motors Center. One was the use of a neoprene gasket weather seal to hold fixed glass and porcelain enamel metal panels to aluminum frames. The sandwiches of glass and porcelain were windproof and waterproof.

197 □

While the Center advanced, Eero worked with his father on Christ Lutheran Church for Minneapolis, Minnesota. Although many projects were carried out jointly with his father, Eero's talent had become increasingly apparent. A fabric-covered, plastic-shell chair he had designed was described in *Life* magazine as inexpensive but comfortable and handsome.

In June, 1949, Yale conferred an M.A. degree on Eero with the citation: "He has won to a position of distinguished leadership . . . while still young enough to eclipse in the future his own achievements of past and present."

The following year, Eliel Saarinen died. Finland gave him an official state funeral. Eero, who had been so close to his father both in personal and professional relationships, was bewildered by the loss. How could he ever come up to the exalted ideals of his father, who had so often reminded him of the necessity to show integrity of mind and spirit?

The need to provide a home for his mother and an office for himself forced Eero to turn away from self-centered grief. For Loja he built a home on land at the back of the Victorian farmhouse. He moved his office into workmanlike but colorful rooms in Bloomfield Hills, a mile from his home.

Possessed by his ideas, Eero often worked far into the night. Because he loved what he was doing, he felt little need for recreation. He and Lily had almost no social life, and if they did go to a party, he usually ended up talking about architecture.

Lily became increasingly disturbed by Eero's concentration on his profession. "You are letting your work devour your life," she said one day. "I thought I was marrying an architect, not architecture."

It was true, Eero thought ruefully, that he took less time for his family than he should. During the next few weeks he tried harder to be a good husband and father. There were moments of closeness to Lily when they shared a common interest in art. He wrestled with ten-year-old Eric and talked to him about mechanics and science. He told stories to pug-nosed, blonde Susan, two years younger than her brother.

But as commissions swamped him, Saarinen once more let architecture take priority on his time. Work went forward on the General Motors Technical Center and on buildings for Drake University in Des Moines, Iowa. One of his most unusual assignments was a temporary shelter big enough to seat large audiences at the annual music festival in the mountain town of Aspen, Colorado. Saarinen designed a tent that spread a vibrant light through the interior.

Even after he had worked hard all day on a design, Saarinen would not stop until midnight. Then, suddenly ravenous, he would go with his partners and close friends, Joseph Lacy and J. Henderson Barr, to a restaurant. Normally his conversation was slow-paced and punctuated by pipe puffs; but when he was excited, he became eloquent. He always argued heatedly in defense of modern architecture but thought buildings should be given some enrichment. To illustrate a point he often drew diagrams on paper napkins.

When Saarinen talked with his friends about projects under way, his conversation was interspersed with *we* instead of *I*. But one night he confided his hope that some of his own buildings would have lasting truth.

This goal of lasting truth made him a better architect, but it increased the strains in family life. He and Lily drifted further apart and finally were divorced. Saarinen had loved his family and felt lost without his wife and children. He could see that there were steps he might have taken to save his marriage, but it was too late now. In the future he must walk alone.

To offset his loneliness, Saarinen drove himself harder than before. On planes and trains, as he crisscrossed the country and checked on projects, he designed and prepared articles and speeches.

199 □

He disliked being away from his drafting table to sit at conference tables and have his designs passed from hand to hand.

These designs were winning widespread attention. In 1953, the vibrant and attractive Mrs. Aline B. Louchheim, who had several times written favorable comments on Saarinen's work, interviewed him for the New York *Times*.

Saarinen felt she was too complimentary in her article about him, but he appreciated her understanding and told her so. As their acquaintanceship developed, Eero found that Aline from the age of nine had been interested in art and architecture. A graduate of Vassar College, she also had an M.A. degree from the Institute of Fine Arts of New York University. She was a divorcée and had two children, Donald and Hal, both in their teens. She missed a normal family life as much as Saarinen did.

The sense of companionship between them impelled Eero to fly to New York to court Aline. He'd never be a satisfactory husband, he told her. He worked like a fiend and he was no handyman around the house. Furthermore, he had to travel a great deal. Aline, who gave much of herself to her writing, understood Eero's consuming love for architecture.

After their marriage in 1954, Eero rebuilt the interior of the old house and converted the garage into a joint study. Nights, while Eero designed, Aline wrote at a desk facing him.

Despite his resolutions to give more attention to home and family, which came to include a young son, Eames, Eero still neglected household chores. Because he put off fixing a leak, a spring thaw poured six inches of water into the basement. But he did let his affection be more evident; and often when he had to be gone, he would leave "I love you" notes taped to the walls to surprise Aline.

Absences became more frequent as Saarinen and his associates built dormitories, chapels, and classroom buildings for a number of campuses—Vassar College, the University of Chicago, Stephens

College at Columbia, Missouri, and Concordia Senior College at Fort Wayne, Indiana. A master plan for the University of Michigan was never carried out.

For Kresge Auditorium at M.I.T., Saarinen had to work on a crowded city campus. He built dozens of models before he came up with a white shell of concrete and a tricornered dome. Asked to do a chapel for the same campus, he planned a cylindrical brick structure with a simple but graceful bell tower. When he got to the lighting, he recalled a night he had spent on a mountain in Sparta. There had been bright moonlight overhead with a hushed secondary light around the horizon. To create a similar effect, he kept the building windowless but introduced light from a honeycomb skylight and also bounced it up through arches rising from water in a moat that surrounded the chapel.

Saarinen had to find expression for a very different function when he designed a War Memorial Center for Milwaukee, Wisconsin. He had accepted the assignment only after he won permission to do a memorial that could be used. The building he evolved was cross-shaped with a bridgehead extending beyond a forty-foot bluff framing the park below and a breathtaking view of Lake Michigan. The first level housed an art museum. An intermediate terrace had a memorial court with names of the war dead inscribed on the granite coping of a pool. Offices and rooms for meetings occupied the top floor.

Another kind of design problem confronted Saarinen in planning a bank for Columbus, Indiana. How could he make his bank look modern and still make it harmonize with the Victorian store fronts it would have as neighbors?

His answer was a one-story building, similar to a pavilion, in the middle of a tree-filled plaza. To break the monotony of the flat roof, he used nine opaque domes of shell concrete. By setting the glass front far back under the roof, he avoided reflection and created a friendly atmosphere. Inside, tellers worked at open windows with gay, varied fronts. After the bank opened in its new building, business quadrupled.

During the time Saarinen had executed all these designs, construction had gone forward on the General Motors Technical Center. When it was dedicated in 1956, some architects said that the water tower and fountains had been called upon to do a work of visual unification that did not come off. One reporter said the Center could best be appreciated if viewed from a speeding car.

But the stainless steel water tower, the dramatic spiral staircase of the Research Administration Building, the rhythmical, glittering expanses of aluminum, greenish glass, and gray porcelain of the façades showed the skill and polish of a bold designer. Although the buildings were similar, Saarinen had given them individuality by doing the end areas in glazed Ohio shale bricks. Each building had a different color. To get bricks that ranged from tangerine and chartreuse to a deep crimson, special kilns had been used for processing.

Architectural Forum called the Technical Center an industrial Versailles. One editor commented, "The Technical Center is an architectural feat that may be unique in our time."

For relaxation between designs and dedications, Saarinen liked to draw cartoons. His young son Eames was an appreciative audience.

Through his sensitivity and understanding, Saarinen gained the confidence of clients almost as easily as that of his son. To him it was only natural that an architect should be as concerned and as involved as his client. He paid relentless attention to detail.

His responsible yet dramatic architecture won him a following. *Time* magazine said none of the younger architects had a better-proportioned combination of good sense, versatility, and imagination than Saarinen.

How had he arrived? young architects asked repeatedly. He an-

□ 202

Over-all view of the General Motors Technical Center, by Eero Saarinen. Photograph courtesy the General Motors Company.

swered this question when he spoke to students at the Illinois Institute of Technology in April, 1956. "You young architects will find the qualities necessary for an architect are humility and crust. Humility for the problem and the realities; crust for solving the problem and sticking with the essentials of the solution."

Buildings, he said, should stimulate man's imagination, give him confidence. To produce that kind of building takes dedication and intuition. Saarinen also stressed individuality, but he did not believe it could be taught. It was, he said, a quality of thinking and depended on the individual's faith, honesty, devotion, and moral integrity.

All the qualities Saarinen recommended to young architects were called into play as he undertook United States Embassies in Oslo and London. These assignments were considered prestige plums, but they presented unusual problems because they involved complexes of offices, official residences, exhibition halls, and libraries. Besides this, the State Department stipulated that the buildings should create an atmosphere of good will and yet express American individuality.

The Embassy site in Oslo faced the Royal palace. Saarinen designed a triangular structure with a façade of precast concrete and rich dark-green Norwegian granite-aggregate. To offset the depressing effect of long, dark winter days, he placed offices around an enclosed court with warm lighting that gave the impression of sunlight. The court had a beige travertine floor, teakwood walls, and brick grille.

For the London Embassy, Saarinen made over two thousand drawings, sometimes running through 170 feet of tracing paper in a single evening. He chose Portland stone for a building material because it would weather to black and white, a color combination that fitted London. To relieve somberness, he used a gold trim. Over the main entrance there was an aluminum eagle with wings outstretched.

Some Londoners said the trim gave the building an aggressive

□ 204

General Motors Technical Center, Administration Building, Warren, Michigan, by Eero Saarinen and Associates. Photograph courtesy The Museum of Modern Art.

hardness. Many criticized the unfriendliness of the waterless moat behind the retaining wall and the metal fence that topped the embankment and separated the building from the sidewalk. But none denied the fine draftsmanship involved. The façade was strong and full of character, and the building won an A.I.A. award of merit.

At the same time the embassies were under way, Saarinen was designing buildings for the Yale campus. The Ingalls Hockey Rink had a hovering entrance that opened into a high luminous interior spanned by a soaring concrete arch that swooped downward at the sides. The remark about it that pleased Saarinen most was made by a goalie on the Yale hockey team. "Go, go, go!" he exclaimed exuberantly, when he saw the rink the first time.

After Saarinen and his associates were asked to design dormitories for Yale, he traveled to England to study housing at Oxford University. Then he went to the Yale campus to get acquainted with the site and the students. Yale students expressed a preference for random, individual rooms.

Saarinen finally decided that each of the dormitories would have its own lounges, library, office, buttery or snack bar, and 250 student rooms in different sizes and shapes. No two buildings would be alike, but they would be unified by courts, terraces, and covered passageways. Saarinen and his associates went through months of trial and error, trying to invent an exterior treatment that would relate the new buildings in color and character with older buildings on the campus.

Eero and his associate and friend John Dinkeloo hit upon a process to make an earthy masonry. This involved placing pieces of crushed granite in wood frames on the wall. A special kind of cement was pumped in through hoses. Before the cement had completely set, the frames were removed and the wall surface was hosed off. Removal of excess cement with chisels and wire brushes exposed the granite.

"They'll make good sturdy ruins," Saarinen quipped when he

saw the work in progress. The press called the dormitories another proof of Saarinen's honesty as a builder.

Between building plans, he squeezed in designs for furniture. Tables and chairs should look like pieces of sculpture, he told Aline. His solution was pedestal furniture, half metal and half plastic. He topped one-legged tables with marble or fine wood. Pedestal chairs had plastic, tulip-shaped seats.

From chairs, Saarinen turned to industrial plants. A smokeless International Business Machines electronics plant outside Rochester, Minnesota, had a sweeping ensemble of rectilinear buildings planned so that additions could be made without looking like warts. Glass curtain walls reflected the landscape, white or green according to the season.

The I.B.M. Corporation was so pleased that they invited Saarinen to do their Thomas J. Watson Research Center in Westchester County, New York, near Yorktown. Saarinen provided a three-story crescent-shaped building of metal, glass, and buff-colored masonry. It sat on the crown of a hill approached by a winding road leading through a hollow past a little lake. The main hallway placed behind the façade was much like the promenade deck of a ship. Short corridors for the use of the scientists had windows at the ends, but research laboratories, where pure air is important, were windowless.

Some praised the thousand-foot-long façade of near-black metal glass as the most majestic of modern times. Others spoke of the building's "robust romanticism."

By 1958, Saarinen headed a seventy-man staff that was rated one of the finest in the world. Kevin Roche, a gifted young architect, was an associate. Joseph Lacy was project manager, and John Dinkeloo, who was in charge of specifications and construction supervision, had become a partner.

The office had the reputation of being a stimulating place in which to work and attracted architects from the Orient, Australia, and South America as well as the United States. Applicants came in droves. To test a young would-be employee, Saarinen would say, "Draw a house or a horse or something." He judged less by the accuracy of the sketch than by the zest shown.

Saarinen gave honesty himself and insisted on it in his associates. He could not understand indifference or shoddiness. Designers and draftsmen who did not share his drive for perfection or who objected to working at their tables half the night when a big project was under way did not stay long. Saarinen drove himself harder than he did his employees. He cluttered the area around his drafting table with discarded skeletons of his own exploration and experiment.

"I wish there weren't so many reasonable ways of getting different solutions," he told Kevin Roche one day.

On designs that he circulated among associates, he made notations such as, "Do you think this is getting too complicated?" or "I still have to think about this."

Office routines were frequently interrupted by the necessity to travel to check on projects. Aline often went with him on extended official trips or short recreational ones. Whether they visited Finland, Greece, Australia, or Thailand, Eero was constantly sketching and taking pictures. From these lands Aline and he brought back art objects—silver Peruvian llamas, a bronze Buddha.

Trips were often punctuated by speech making. If Saarinen had an audience of architects, he appealed to them to contribute beauty. "There is too much in the world that is ugly," he told them. To members of the American Institute of Architects, he said it was important to look back now and then at the architecture of other times and test today's achievements against past. "It is a terribly good way," he said, "to knock the pins out from under our smugness." He urged architects not to use the same formula over and over. "We must explore and expand our horizons," he told them.

In an address at Dickinson College, Saarinen said architecture must make an emotional impact on man. Architecture, he stated, had an almost religious role, and religion gives man his primary purpose. "So to the question, what is the purpose of architecture, I would answer, To shelter and enhance man's life on earth and to fulfill his belief in the nobility of existence."

Saarinen practiced the enhancement he talked about when he designed a headquarters for John Deere and Company at Moline, Illinois. The plant would be located in a wooded ravine overlooking a man-made lake. The façade of the main building would be glass and Cor-ten steel which in two years would turn to a cinnamon brown. Windows would have sun-shading louvers and laminated mirror glass that reflected heat away. Buildings would be connected by glass-enclosed bridges.

Saarinen and Associates were at the same time designing the Bell Telephone Laboratories Engineering and Development Center at Holmdel, New Jersey. It would have a staff of forty-five hundred scientists, making it one of the largest research centers in the world. When the first glass and steel building in the complex was completed, it was described as a gleaming scientific instrument in itself.

While the Bell Laboratory Building was under construction, Saarinen was also designing a handsome Law School for the University of Chicago and a fifteen-million-dollar Terminal Building for Trans-World Airlines at what is now Kennedy International Airport. The TWA project had been on his drafting board for months, but he kept changing his plans. He was determined to get away from the ugliness, and inconveniences of many of the terminals he had visited.

Saarinen had an important site for the TWA Building, opposite the main entrance to the airport. But he worried about how he could build a structure that would be dramatic and yet be related to the glistening complex of low-lying buildings already there. And he wasn't sure how he could best serve passengers.

"I want the traveler to feel uplifted and to catch the excitement of the trip," he told Aline.

One morning at breakfast, his mind centered on the problem

of a roof for the TWA Building. Instead of eating his grapefruit, he carved it into elliptical, parabolic arches. When he left for the office, he took the grapefruit with him to serve as a model. It led to a design with a reinforced concrete roof composed of four intersecting barrel shells or vaults of slightly different shapes that would provide a protective umbrella over the passenger area. The shells would rest on Y-shaped columns and would be connected to one another by a skylight band. The interior would have glass walls and a great vaulted space where continually changing curves would give the impression of motion. Passengers would board planes and disembark via telescoping bridges.

Even after TWA officials accepted the plan, Saarinen and Kevin Roche spent endless hours patterning, cutting, folding, and sculpturing cardboard and wire. As the building rose, it took on somewhat the appearance of a great bird in flight. Inside the building, everything from stairways to the information desk with its marble inlaid top had continuously changing curves that gave the impression of constant motion.

While he was working on the TWA Building, Saarinen was also moving ahead on the government-owned Dulles International Airport for Washington, D.C., at Chantilly, Virginia. Before he began drawings for the terminal, Saarinen worked with consulting engineers Ammann and Whitney, airport consultant Charles Landrum, and mechanical engineers Burns and McDonnell, analyzing the special problems of jet planes. From the first, Saarinen insisted that since the airport was a national and international gateway to our nation, it should be dignified, free from any hint of a honky-tonk.

The roof he designed looked like a concrete hammock suspended between rows of substantial but graceful columns. It would be supported by suspension bridge cables and concrete piers sloping outward to counteract the pull of the cables. On the first level, with its shops and ticker counters, travelers would be able to look out on lawns and lakes.

□ 210

TWA Terminal at Kennedy International Airport, New York City, by Eero Saarinen. Photograph by Ezra Stoller Associates.

Saarinen wanted to find a way to get passengers from terminal to plane without the use of lengthy radial sheds. Often when he had arrived dead tired at a terminal, it had irritated him to have to walk great distances while he lugged architectural plans and briefcases. To document distances and the time consumed in traversing them, Saarinen sent out researchers with stopwatches and counting clickers.

Mobile lounges to cover the distance between the terminal building and the planes seemed best to meet the needs of passengers. Saarinen designed what he called parlor chairs on stilts. His luxurious mobile lounge with tinted windows would seat ninety passengers and could be driven from either end. Such lounges would be expensive, so Saarinen would have to sell the idea to the Federal Aviation Agency and to officials of the dozen airlines operating out of the Dulles Airport.

His friend Charles Eames suggested using a movie. He and Eero devised a ten-minute cartoon film with a sound track that featured the clomp of tired feet. Officials gave Saarinen the go-ahead for his lounge.

Whenever he could be away from Dulles or other sites, he worked in Birmingham, Michigan, where he had moved his office. Saarinen tried to get home early enough to do things with his son Eames. After dinner, Eero sketched or made long lists of activities for the following day. Around eleven o'clock, he and Aline would take a break, during which they had long, wonderful conversations. Sometimes Aline would read aloud her day's production of prose or Eero would share an idea for a new design.

Saarinen's designs had become more mature, more poetic, and were receiving increasing recognition. *Holiday* magazine called him "perhaps the nation's top architect"; *Vogue* referred to him as one of the most famous architects in the world. In 1958, when *Time* magazine asked five hundred architects to choose the Seven Wonders of

American architecture, Saarinen's General Motors Technical Center shared first-place honors with Rockefeller Center.

He was a member of the Congrès Internationaux d'Architecture Moderne and of the American Society of Planners and Architects. In an international competition for a design for a building for the World Health Organization, his entry won second place. Universities at home and abroad conferred honorary doctorates. The Boston Arts Festival gave him their Grand Architectural Award.

Saarinen was both humble and proud when honors came his way. His success, he said, was much due to the influence of his father. In recent years his work had improved because his personal happiness had been bolstered by a remarkably compatible marriage.

Publicity and awards made Saarinen more than ever in demand as a public speaker. He talked more about values than about materials and techniques. In the course of a speech given in Munich he said, "Compromise and confusion are qualities alien to good interiors, just as they are alien to good architecture and good people."

While construction was going forward on the TWA and Dulles Airport Terminal Buildings, Saarinen was designing an airport for Athens, Greece, planned so the entrance would face the field instead of the city. To make it fit with old classical buildings in Athens, he would use white concrete and marble.

Saarinen's first commission for a skyscraper came from the Columbia Broadcasting System. From the outset he thought in terms of a dark tower with light and air around it. In March, 1961, he sent word to Dr. Frank Stanton, President of C.B.S., that he had a good scheme for the headquarters building. "Its beauty, will be, I believe," wrote Saarinen, "that it will be the simplest skyscraper statement in New York."

Saarinen's design was as simple as he had promised it would be. A rectangular shaft supported by triangular piers stood straight and free from the ground and soared to the thirty-eighth floor in a

vertical leap of masonry and glass. The piers would be of reinforced concrete faced with black granite to give elegance. Windows would have dark glass. Supplies would be delivered via a subterranean passage connecting the skyscraper to the utility building next door.

As Saarinen thought, redesigned, juggled parts, it seemed to him like a three-dimensional chess game. Somehow he must make it what Louis Sullivan had said a skyscraper ought to be—a proud and soaring thing.

"I am excited about the C.B.S. Building," he told Aline.

But he was almost equally excited about the Vivian Beaumont Theater in the Lincoln Center for the Performing Arts in New York. On this project, Saarinen and his associates worked with Gordon Bunshaft and other architects affiliated with Skidmore, Owings, and Merrill. Although so many architects were involved, there was no clash of wills, and the plan that emerged called for a vigorously boned concrete structure.

At the same time, Saarinen was involved in plans for the School of Music at the University of Michigan. He conceived of the building as brick inside and out, nestled against a wooded hillside with one three-story rampart extending down a terraced slope to a pool. Pairs of long, slender, dark-tinted windows would look much like the keys of a piano.

For the Michigan project, Saarinen could work out of his home office, but, because so many important commissions were coming up in the East, it seemed wise to plan for an office in that area. He chose a site at Hamden, Connecticut, where he found an old orange-brick mansion that could be remodeled.

While he was still planning for the move, Saarinen visited Dulles Airport. When he was two miles away, the white splendor of the terminal building greeted him. This, he told himself, was the best thing he had ever done. Later, to a reporter, he said unpretentiously, "Maybe it will even explain what I believe about architecture."

215 □

C.B.S. Building, New York City, by Eero
Saarinen. Photograph courtesy C.B.S.

What he believed he had never been able to state adequately, but he had come close to it when he had written for the *Architectural Record,* "Whatever the expression of architecture may be, its roots should be in life itself—the way the building is used and a love for the people who use it."

In August of 1961, Saarinen had a number of buildings in progress, but he lacked energy to do what needed to be done. Aline urged him to go to the University of Michigan Medical Center for a checkup. On the twenty-first of August, the day after his fifty-second birthday, he underwent surgery for a malignant brain tumor. He died two weeks later.

Saarinen had been at the height of his creative powers, and the abruptness with which his life ended dazed and shocked his colleagues. Because he was a perfectionist and searched where others did not care to search, this virtuoso architect left noble legacies in stone, glass, and concrete. With poetic inventiveness he enriched many of his buildings with a kind of sculpture and dramatized them with a daring use of light, color, and materials.

After Saarinen's death, *Christian Century* commented, "Greater than any or all of his creations was this man, this builder."

"This man, this builder," designed his life with the same fierce attention he gave to his buildings. He had inflexible integrity—in his will he stipulated that his name should not be attached to any building he had not designed personally. And Charles Eames said of him that he had the strength of a man who didn't have to pretend. His integrity was bulwarked by fortitude, humility, commitment, and courage.

Besides his finished projects, there were major ones Saarinen did not live to see completed. Among them were the C.B.S. Building, Dulles Airport, the Yale buildings, the Jefferson Memorial Arch, the TWA Building, an airport in Athens, the Bell Laboratories, the the theater in Lincoln Center, and the Music School for the University of Michigan.

Saarinen's three surviving partners—Joseph Lacy, John Dinke-loo, Kevin Roche—pledged themselves to carry out his designs to the best of their ability.

"We are dedicated," said Lacy, "to continuing the practice of architecture according to the high standards of integrity and idealism which he set."

As Saarinen had planned, they moved the office to Connecticut. One by one, the projects have been completed. The Dulles Airport Terminal has been described as an "epochal monument" by Lewis Mumford, an authoritative writer on architecture. Mumford added that it might have been fashioned by Michelangelo. Edgar Kaufmann, Jr., design critic and chief of the Museum of Modern Art's Industrial Design Department, characterized the TWA Building as one of the peaks of modern architecture.

At dedication ceremonies for the School of Music at the University of Michigan, President Harlan H. Hatcher said, "I think it is by all odds one of the most graceful and beautiful creations to be found on any college campus anywhere in the world."

The C.B.S. Building, often referred to as Saarinen's Dark Tower, became the proud and soaring thing he wanted it to be. For the excellence of these and other buildings, the American Institute of Architects presented Aline Saarinen with its Gold Medal of Honor in memory of Eero.

But the award honored a man as well as a builder. For Eero Saarinen was a good man, perhaps even a great men, who wrought more than most.

GLOSSARY

AGGREGATE: That which, added to cement and water, makes concrete. Fine sand or coarse gravel may be added.

A.I.A.: American Institute of Architects.

ARABESQUE: A decorative pattern containing animal, plant, or, occasionally human forms; a decorative pattern of interlaced lines or bands in geometric form—developed in Arabian design.

BAY: Portion of a plan or of a building contained between adjacent piers or columns; a bay window.

CANTILEVER: A projecting beam or girder supported only at one end; a large bracket, usually ornamental, for supporting a balcony.

CIAM: Congrès Internationaux d' Architecture Moderne; International Congress of Modern Building.

COPING: The covering or top used on walls for protection, usually where roof and side walls meet, it may be a projection at top of a wall and is often decorative as well as protective.

CURTAIN WALL: A thin wall, between and often in front of the main structural members of steel or of reinforced concrete, that bears no load.

FAÇADE: The face or front of a building.

FRIEZE: In a paneled room, the space between the top of the paneling and the ceiling; in rooms with papered walls, the space between the picture rail and the ceiling—sometimes decorated.

GRILLE: A grating, openwork, or lattice, usually of metal but sometimes of wood, used to screen or shield an open door or window —often ornamental and decorative.

I BEAM: A steel beam whose cross section resembles the letter I, used in structural work.

JALOUSIE: A blind or shutter with fixed or movable slats—the slats slope so they may admit air and light but keep out sun or rain.

LOUVER: A slatted opening used for ventilation; narrow openings between slats serve as outlets for heated air.

MOTIF: The dominant or distinctive feature or element of design.

MULLION: A vertical bar of stone, wood, or iron in a window frame, separating the window lights; a division between multiple windows.

PAVILION: A partially enclosed structure, usually roofed, to give shelter at the seaside, in parks, or in gardens—light and ornamental in style, it is sometimes adorned with designs.

PEDIMENT: A decorative feature finishing the gable end of a building; also, a triangular, segmental, or ornamented feature over a door or window opening.

PIER: A pillar supporting an arch; a supporting section of wall between two openings; an auxiliary mass of masonry used to strengthen a wall.

PILASTER: A rectangular column attached to a wall or pier, projecting slightly from a wall, structurally serving as a pier but architecturally treated as a column.

PODIUM: The platform on which a building is placed.

PORTICO: A structure consisting of a roof supported by columns, usually attached to a building as a porch.

REINFORCED CONCRETE: Concrete that has been strengthened by iron or steel rods or bars embedded in it.

RELIEF: The slight projection of a figure.

SOFFIT: The finished underside of an arch or other spanning member, usually overhead.

SELECTED BIBLIOGRAPHY

BOOKS

Blake, Peter, *The Master Builders.* New York: Alfred A. Knopf, Inc., 1960. Includes material on Mies van der Rohe and Frank Lloyd Wright.

Drexler, Arthur, *Ludwig Mies van der Rohe.* New York: George Braziller, Inc., 1960. Good analysis of work and good pictorial material; biographical material sparse.

Fitch, James Marston, *Walter Gropius.* New York: George Braziller, Inc., 1960.

Giedion, Sigfried S., *Walter Gropius Work and Teamwork.* New York: Reinhold Publishing Corporation, 1954.

Johnson, Philip C., *Mies van der Rohe.* New York: The Museum of Modern Art, 1947.

McCoy, Esther, *Richard Neutra.* New York: George Braziller, Inc., 1960.

Neutra, Richard, *Life and Shape.* New York: Appleton-Century-Crofts, Inc., 1962. Includes much autobiographical data: one of the most important sources of information.

Saarinen, Eero, edited by Aline B. Saarinen, *Eero Saarinen on His Work.* New Haven and London: Yale University Press, 1962. Profusely illustrated. Statements by the architect.

Stone, Edward D., *The Evolution of an Architect.* New York: Horizon Press, Inc., 1962. A detailed and lively autobiography.

Temko, Allan, *Eero Saarinen.* New York: George Braziller, Inc., 1962.

Whittick, Arnold, *Eric Mendelsohn.* London: Leonard Hill Limited, 1940.

Wright, Olgivanna Lloyd, *The Shining Brow.* New York: Horizon Press, Inc., 1960. Behind-the-scenes glimpses of the architect, written by the architect's wife. The best source on Wright is his own writings.

ARTICLES

There are dozens of magazine articles on the architects. The best procedure for the student interested in a particular architect would be to consult the *Reader's Guide to Periodical Literature* or *Current Biography*. Two articles of special interest to younger readers are:

Stone, Edward D., as told to Charlotte Willard, "Architecture—My Way of Life." *Boy's Life,* March, 1965, pp. 22–24.

Clark, Blake, "America's Unconventional Master Builder." *Reader's Digest,* February, 1965, pp. 192–196.

About the Author

Aylesa Forsee writes: "While teaching in high schools and universities and acting as counselor at a Y-Teen Camp, I became deeply interested in teen-agers and their potentialities. It was inevitable after exchanging teaching for writing that I should put out books which I hope will challenge some who read them to build the kind of life they dream about. I am not one of those writers who can point with pride to a novel or a play penned at a tender age, having come to writing the long way round."

During Miss Forsee's childhood, spent mostly in Brookings, South Dakota, where her father was a physician, favorite pastimes were music, winter sports, Girl Scouting, camping, and reading. Violin was her great love, but a late start made a musical career impractical. So at South Dakota State College she majored in science and social science, later picking up a Bachelor of Music degree at the MacPhail College of Music and a Master of Arts degree at the University of Colorado. Sandwiched in with teaching in Minnesota was participation in the Rochester Civic Symphony and the Duluth Symphony.

Miss Forsee's present home is in Boulder, Colorado, where she takes time out from her writing to go picnicking and camping in the Rockies and pursues her musical interest by playing in the Boulder Philharmonic Orchestra.

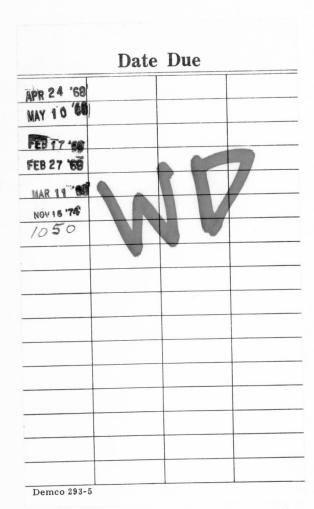